WHAT'S THE ISSUE?

JAN / / 2020

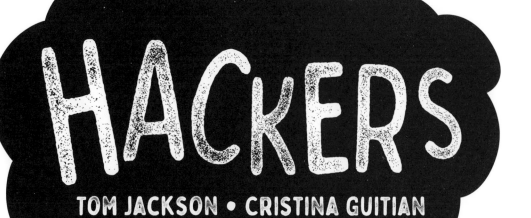

HACKERS

TOM JACKSON • CRISTINA GUITIAN

QEB

Quarto is the authority on a wide range of topics.

Quarto educates, entertains and enriches the lives of our readers—enthusiasts and lovers of hands-on living.

www.quartoknows.com

Author: Tom Jackson
Illustrator: Cristina Guitian
Designers: Tracy Killick and Mike Henson
Editors: Claire Watts and Ellie Brough
Editorial Director: Laura Knowles
Creative Director: Malena Stojic
Publisher: Maxime Boucknooghe

First published in 2019 by QEB Publishing,
an imprint of The Quarto Group.
6 Orchard Road, Suite 100, Lake Forest, CA 92630.
T +1 949 380 7510
F +1 949 380 7575
www.QuartoKnows.com

A CIP record for this book is available from the Library of Congress.

ISBN 978 0 7112 4458 0

Manufactured in Guangdong, China CC082019
9 8 7 6 5 4 3 2 1

CONTENTS

Words in **bold** are explained
in the glossary on page 92.

AUTHOR'S NOTE

WHAT'S THE ISSUE WITH HACKING?

It's a complicated subject, but never fear because
you are in the right place to find out. I can't give
you any simple answers, I'm afraid, but this book
will help you figure out for yourself what you
think about hacking. All I can do is tell you what I
know and set out what's what and who's who.

THEN IT'S UP TO YOU TO MAKE AN INFORMED OPINION.

Hacking and the online world are expanding into all areas of
our life; into art, money, politics and crime, and into the way
we communicate. It sounds like something you need to know
about. In this book, I'll break it down for you, but even then,
the wrongs and rights of hacking are not always clear. Every
now and then, you'll get a chance to question what you've
read and think about it.

WHAT DO YOU THINK?
WHAT DO YOUR FRIENDS THINK?
WHAT DO YOUR PARENTS THINK?
WHAT DOES YOUR TEACHER THINK?

Everyone and anyone can have an opinion, but not everyone's
will be informed. With this book, you will have the knowledge
to back up your arguments.

OPINIONS MATTER, SO WHAT WILL YOURS BE?

WHAT IS A HACKER?

Do you know a hacker? Are you one yourself? (Is that a secret?) Computer hacking is an intriguing subject, but what is it and what are its effects? Hackers in films and on TV lurk in dark rooms, typing really fast. They are mostly strange, shy characters and are seldom the hero of the story. In real life, the faces of real hackers stare out from news stories about serious crimes where secrets or money have been stolen. So, are hackers always freaky, creepy, or crooked? Let's find out.

NAME IT

To understand hacking, it's best to start with the origin of the word. "Hack" means to cut up roughly. It was first used in the modern sense in 1955—not in relation to computers but to model railways! The members of the Tech Model Railroad Club at the Massachusetts Institute of Technology (MIT), were coming up with ways of getting more power to the tracks and kept making rapid and rough changes while trains were running—often overloading the circuits. This was called hacking, and these model train enthusiasts were the first hackers. The term "hacker" came to refer to a person who messes around with technology to see if they can get it to work better or in other ways—but who may break it in the process.

MIT's Tech Model Railroad Club began after World War II. As well as building track, modeling landscapes, and painting carriages, its members wanted to build a computer control system for the impressive model railway. They had access to some of the biggest and best computers in the world, and so hacking the railway led to hacking computers too. At MIT today, a hack is also a prank using buildings, furniture, or other student facilities. Although they are against the rules at MIT, this kind of hacking is tolerated because it encourages students to think differently about things.

DEFINING HACKERS

By 1975, computer scientists had invented a whole new language, which they recorded in the Jargon File: a list of tech slang. The Jargon File defined 'hacker' in several different ways. Here are the main ones:

A person who enjoys exploring the details of programmable systems and how to stretch their capabilities, as opposed to most users, who prefer to learn only the minimum necessary.

A person who likes to spend time and effort solving a problem that has no obvious value, and enjoys the challenge of getting around limits and rules.

An expert or enthusiast of any kind.

A malicious meddler who tries to discover sensitive information by poking around—also known as a cracker.

THE WAY AHEAD

So hackers are creative and clever, they bend the rules and figure out new ways of doing things. Hacking is not confined to computers and communications—people hack genes, hack engineering, and hack life itself. Hackers need not be the bad guys either. Many of today's top tech developers started out as hackers. However, our attention is generally on the crackers—the harmful hackers. If we drop our guard, sooner or later they'll get us. We need to understand more about that.

KEEPING SECRETS

The rise of the hacker has gone hand-in-hand with the rise of digital technology. The convenience of this tech has had a big effect on the way we live. We are able to buy and sell whatever we want with a few clicks, and we can share our lives with loved ones as if we were all in the same room. However, to do that, we need to keep secrets. Secret passwords and information keep our digital lives private and safe. How do we stop those secrets from falling into the wrong hands?

SECRET WRITING

Okay, everyone has secrets. Each secret is a problem to solve. Is it right to keep it or should I share it? This is something people struggle with throughout their lives. However, digital secrets pose a different problem entirely. We have to share them with others to use our online services but make sure people who are not involved in the transaction can't watch. Fortunately there is a long history of communicating in secret using a system called cryptography, which means "secret writing." Cryptography is the first line of defense against a hacker.

CODES

The simplest kind of cryptography is a code—simple in that it is easy to set up, but not necessarily easy to crack. The word "code" is often used to mean any way of hiding the true meaning of a message, but more correctly a code is a system where

the meaning is hidden by changing entire words. Here's a coded message: "This orange is blue!" It could mean absolutely anything. You can only find out for sure by using a codebook, which lists code words and their true meaning. In this code, "orange" means "book" and "blue" means "amazing"—it's obvious once you know!

CODE TALKERS

The United States military used a special team of code experts in the world wars. Native American radio operators used codes based on their languages, such as Comanche, Navajo, and Cherokee. Even if the enemy—mostly German or Japanese speakers—listened in to the radio signals, they had no idea what any of it meant or how to even begin to figure it out.

IDIOT CODE

The simplest type of code—so easy to understand an idiot could do it—is the hardest to break. The trick is to use it only once or twice, and then set up a new one. An "idiot code" can only send a few kinds of message, such as "Meet at Location Z." "Meet" could be coded by referring to an animal. The location is given in the sentence. "We saw a fox in the park today. I think it's the same one we saw at Location Z."

There is a problem with codes, as summed up by Benjamin Franklin, the great American scientist and statesman. He said, "Three people can keep a secret if two of them are dead." What he meant was that it is very easy to reveal secrets. For a code to work, every user needs a codebook. If the book fell into the wrong hands, the entire code is revealed. In World War II, the German Navy printed their codebooks using water soluble ink. If the books fell overboard, their secrets would just wash away.

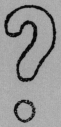

TO ENCRYPT OR NOT TO ENCRYPT?

Encryption is the act of making something into a secret. There are many ways to do it, but should we encrypt all our messages and information? When does it make sense to use secrecy, and when might it be a good idea to keep things public?

9

CIPHERS

Serious cryptography, the kind used by armies, spies, and online services, uses a system called a cipher. While codes hide meaning by transforming words, a cipher does it by transforming individual letters. The original message is called the plaintext and the encrypted version is the ciphertext. To convert plaintext to ciphertext requires a set of instructions called the key. To decrypt the message, the same key is used but applied in reverse. A key is best organized as a list of mathematical processes. That way it is impossible to get things muddled. As we'll see, these instructions can be very simple—but also so complex that a supercomputer could not figure them out in a billion years (or can they...?).

CAESAR CIPHER

One of the simplest ciphers was used by Julius Caesar, the warring dictator of Rome. It is a substitution cipher: each letter in the alphabet is replaced by another letter a fixed number of positions further along the alphabet. So if the cipher key was +1, the plaintext "ABCD" would be encrypted as "BCDE"—HFU JU? A negative number key means you go in the other direction. The alphabet forms a continuous loop, so once you get to Z, you start again at A. To decrypt you just switch the sign of the key, so + 1 becomes - 1: "HFU JU?" reads as "GET IT?"

PUBLIC AND PRIVATE

A cipher key is easier to keep secret than a codebook, but it still needs to be exchanged. This is the weakest part of the process. The chance of the key being discovered increases each time it's passed

A set of instructions, such as a cipher key, that is designed to convert one thing into another is called an **algorithm**. The word algorithm comes from the name Al-Khwarizmi. This Persian guy, who invented **algebra** (an Arabic word) in the 9th century, was often called "Algorithmi" in European books. This proves that codes and cipher are really about math. The best hackers understand the importance of being good at sums.

on to a new person. To be safest, you must meet in person and whisper the key into their ear. Modern communications allow us to talk with people we have never met, and never will. So we have to use a system where we can exchange private encryption keys in full view of everyone, but in a way that they'll never know what it is. Hackers know how that system works. Later on you'll find out too (see page 28).

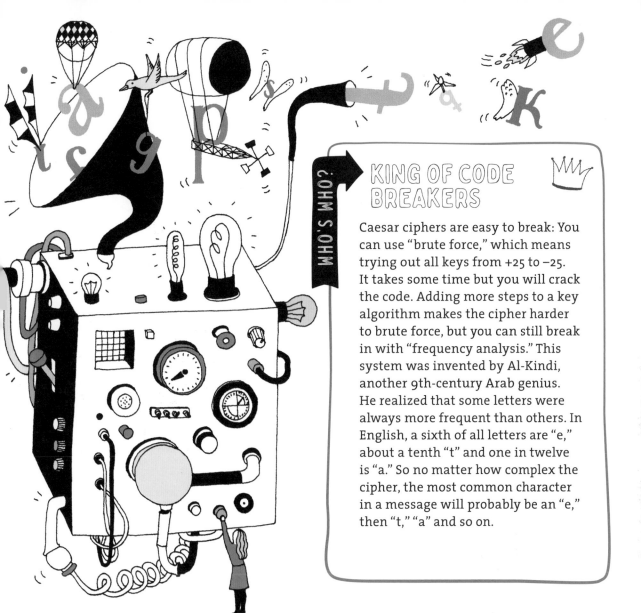

WHO'S OHM?

KING OF CODE BREAKERS

Caesar ciphers are easy to break: You can use "brute force," which means trying out all keys from +25 to −25. It takes some time but you will crack the code. Adding more steps to a key algorithm makes the cipher harder to brute force, but you can still break in with "frequency analysis." This system was invented by Al-Kindi, another 9th-century Arab genius. He realized that some letters were always more frequent than others. In English, a sixth of all letters are "e," about a tenth "t" and one in twelve is "a." So no matter how complex the cipher, the most common character in a message will probably be an "e," then "t," "a" and so on.

WHAT WOULD YOU DO WITH A CODE?

If you invented a super secure cipher, what would you do with it? Keeping it secret would mean that you could communicate in private. But making it public would mean that no one else could use it, because everyone could read the messages. Some hackers like to break **encryption** so they can see private messages, while others make the keys public, so it's harder for people to keep dangerous secrets. What would you do?

TELECOMS

In the old days, if you wanted to talk to a friend, you had to send them a letter or see them in person. Now we use telecommunication, which allows us to have long-distance conversations. This doesn't just mean phones and computers—telecommunications is much older than that! As it has evolved, so have hackers, continuing the centuries' old battle for secure messages.

Pardon?

WRITTEN WORD

The first long-distance communication form was the letter. To prove their identity, each sender would use a uniquely patterned "seal." The ancient Mesopotamians rolled a cylindrical seal onto wet clay. By the Middle Ages, Europeans were "sealing" their letters with wax, pressing an identifying pattern into it. Once opened, it could not be re-sealed without destroying the wax seal, so it couldn't be read secretly by someone else en route. You can hack wax, though, with a hot knife and a steady hand.

Sealing wax is a little bit like **quantum** cryptography, a futuristic security system. It is impossible to hack this system without giving yourself away (see page 85.) There's no hot knife hack for this system yet.

HIGHER SPEEDS

Letters are very slow: today's post takes a couple of days, but in the past it took months. Visual communication, like smoke signals, is much faster. They carried simple meanings, such as "Attack!" or "Victory!"

From this, flag-based signal systems called semaphore were developed, where letters were represented by the positions of two flags. In the 1790s, a network of semaphore towers was built across France. They could transmit short messages at 300 miles per hour in good weather. This was the first high-speed telecom system—and it was the first to be hacked (see page 18).

FIBER OPTICS

Today's telecommunications are sent along optical fibers: flexible strands of glass bundled together. The message is encoded as flickering pulses of laser light, which shine in one end of the strand and then reflect off the inside wall of the glass, bouncing to the other end. The messages travel at the speed of light: fast enough to go around the world seven times in one second. So messages today can go anywhere on Earth in an instant.

WIRED COMMUNICATION

The 19th century saw the rise of systems that sent messages along electrified wires. The first form was the telegraph: a pair of switches connected by miles of wire. If you closed the switch at one end of the wire, it also closed the switch at the other end, making a buzz or click. Samuel Morse concocted his famous code of long and short clicks to send wire messages. Telegraph means "distance writing," and telephone means "distance talking." The telephone was a later invention, where the sound wave of the voice was converted into a corresponding electrical wave for transmission along wires. Telephone technology appeared in the 1860s and a century later it formed the foundation of digital communications.

IS ALL COMMUNICATION EQUAL?

Since the first postal systems started in Mesopotamia around 2,500 years ago, private messages have been protected by law. It is illegal to access someone else's letters, voicemails, emails, or text messages. Do we use different methods to send different kinds of messages? Does that mean some message types are more important, and more private, than others?

CODE BREAKERS

Code breakers have played many pivotal roles throughout history, both starting and ending wars. Here are some code breakers who have made history.

In the late 16th century, France was at war with Spain. The war showed no sign of ending until a mathematician called François Viète got involved. He decrypted the Spanish force's secret military orders and the two sides were forced to make peace.

KILLER QUEENS

In the 1560s, Queen Elizabeth I of England imprisoned her Catholic cousin Mary I of Scotland because she feared that she might usurp the English throne. When Mary's letters to her conspirators were discovered, Elizabeth's cryptographer, Thomas Phelippes, decoded them to reveal her plot. Mary used a homophonic cipher, where one plaintext letter was shown by several possible ciphertext symbols. It was also a nomenclator system, where frequently used names—Elizabeth, Mary, Spain—had their own symbols. This made frequency analysis difficult. It took Phelippes several months to break in, but he did so by identifying common English phrases. For example, letters generally start and end in the same way: "Dear..." and "Yours...," so he started here and found out that Mary wanted King Philip of Spain to invade England and kill Elizabeth. Once the code was cracked, Mary was executed.

TELEGRAM HACK

In 1917, the United States was considering joining World War I (1914–18) as France and Britain's ally. The German foreign minister sent a telegram (a letter sent via telegraph) to Mexico asking them to invade the United States to stop US troops from coming to Europe. In return, Mexico would get back Texas and other territories the United States had taken. The Germans couldn't send messages to Mexico (all the telegraph cables went via Britain) but they could send a few coded signals to the United States. These coded messages were meant for peace talks, but the Germans tricked an American official into sending on the Mexican telegram, still hidden by its code. Today's hackers use a similar technique called a Trojan Horse to hide malicious deeds inside a seemingly useful task (see more on page 31). The Mexicans refused to join the Germans' side. In any case British spies had soon decoded the message and warned the Americans. However, they had to invent a story about how they got hold of it so that the Americans would not realize the British were spying on the US telegrams as well!

WHAT'S WHAT?

THE ENIGMA CODE

By World War II, the German military was using the Enigma machine. In some ways, this encryption machine was very simple. It was a keyboard linked to a set of light bulbs (one for each letter). When you pressed a key, a bulb lit up. The cipher was also homophonic: one letter could be encoded into any other letter. Each bulb was controlled by a system of cogs and electric wiring, which were set up differently every day so there were 158,962,555,217,826,360,000 possible ciphers to choose from!

WHO'S WHO?

ALAN TURING

The Enigma code was supposedly unbreakable, but it was flawed like earlier codes. The messages often ended with "Heil Hitler," and weather reports were sent at the same time each day. These plaintext words and phrases were used to crack the ciphertext. A team of cryptographers led by Alan Turing built the Bombe, a computer-like machine that tried out every possible combination for short phrases until it matched that day's ciphertext. Job done!

CODE READ, WHAT NEXT?

Cracking codes leads to a dilemma. Do you act on what you have discovered in the code—and reveal that the code is no longer secret—or do you keep quiet and keep listening in?

Shhh...

DOES THAT COMPUTE?

Alan Turing is remembered as a codebreaker who helped to win World War II and save countless lives. That is quite an achievement until you realize that what Turing also did was invent the digital computer. Without Turing, hackers might not even exist!

THE VIRTUAL MACHINE

Turing's work on computers was a bit of an accident. As a mathematician, he was looking for an answer to a complicated problem about algorithms. Some algorithms always produce a final answer (what that is is not important) and some algorithms just keep going forever. Turing wanted to know if there was a way of telling one from the other without having to try them all out. To investigate, he used an imaginary, or "virtual," machine that could follow any algorithm and remember the results. Does this virtual machine sound familiar? It took a few years for technology to catch up, but the designs of the first digital computers were based on Turing's virtual machine.

And the answer to Turing's algorithm question? Can you test algorithms to see if they have an end point? Er… no, you can't.

COMPUTER PIONEERS

Computers existed long before Turing. "Computer" was the name for people whose job it was to do very complicated math. Several people had tried to build mechanical calculators that could do the work of a human computer. The most successful was Charles Babbage. In 1837, Babbage designed the Analytical Engine, a mechanical device that had a programmable processor (called the Mill) and a memory (the Store) which could hold a thousand 50-digit numbers! It would have been the first general purpose computer if only Babbage could have afforded to make all 25,000 separate parts!

ADA LOVELACE

Ada Lovelace showed Babbage how the Analytical Engine could be programmed to do fiendishly complex calculations, and so she is remembered as the first computer programmer.

BITS AND BYTES

Claude Shannon introduced the idea of a "**bit**" of information in 1948. It's short for binary digit and represents a single digit, a 1 or a 0, in a computer's memory, processor, or program. Later a useful chunk, or bite, of 8 bits became known as a **byte** (the spelling was changed to avoid confusion). Half a byte—4 bits—is called a nibble.

LOGIC CIRCUITS

A computer uses a kind of math called Boolean algebra, which uses 1s and 0s, and has weird rules, such as 1+1 = 1. A computer's circuits follow these rules, so it can be used to perform acts of logic, or make simple decisions, such as yes or no, true or false, on or off. Deep down that is all a computer is doing, billions of times a second. The American mathematician Claude Shannon devised electrical systems based on Boolean algebra around the same time as Alan Turing was imagining his machine. The first computer to have both Turing's system—a **processor**, program, and memory—and Shannon's logic circuits was the Manchester Baby, built in Manchester in 1948.

WHAT IS INFORMATION FOR?

The amount of information available only ever goes up, as we learn and record more about the world. What is this information for? Is it to make us smart, to make money, or is it just a by-product of the human mind?

THE FIRST HACKERS

Being able to communicate over long distances has revolutionized society, that's for sure. And it has also revolutionized the way we cheat and steal! The first high-speed telecoms system was a network of semaphore towers built in the early 19th century across Europe—and that was also used for the first hack! Let's look at a brief history of hacking to get us up to date.

At the turn of the 20th century, Italian Guglielmo Marconi developed a brand new way to communicate— radio. Radio messages traveled as invisible waves and did not need wires like a telegram. Marconi even demonstrated that radio could send a signal all the way across the Atlantic. Today, the exact same radio waves form the basis of all wireless communications from TV broadcasts to Bluetooth and mobile phones.

1834 SEMAPHORE HACK

Francois and Joseph Blanc developed a way of hiding secret information inside the official code sent via semaphore. The brothers led a small team of hackers to transmit sensitive stock market information from Paris to Bordeaux so they could know about price changes before anyone else—and get rich quick! The scam ran for two years before someone snitched, but no one went to prison because hacking communications systems was not against the law yet.

DOUBLE AGENT

Computer expert René Carmille worked for the Germans in World War II, programming machines that recorded who lived in France, including Jewish people who were to be sent to death camps. Carmille was actually working for the Resistance. He sabotaged the cards used to input data, so the machines didn't record Jewish heritage. His hack was discovered, and he died in one of the camps that he had saved so many others from.

NETWORKING

In 1940, mathematician George Stibitz was working on very early versions of the electronic calculator. The processor that did the number-crunching was a separate machine from the keyboard used to type in sums. Stibitz decided to connect the two by a telephone wire and in doing so created the first computer network.

1903 SCIENTIFIC HOOLIGAN

In 1903, Marconi performed a demonstration to show that his radio equipment could be finely tuned so only a receiver set to the same frequency could pick up the signal. Marconi owned the patent for radio, so no one else was allowed to use the technology. During Marconi's demonstration, Nevil Maskelyne, a magician who used radio in his act, took over with a more powerful signal, tapping out the words "rats, rats, rats" in Morse. Marconi described the attack as "scientific hooliganism."

1956 PHREAKING

Josef Engressia, nicknamed Joybubbles, had perfect pitch, meaning he could whistle any note without being guided by a musical instrument. In the late 1950s, while still a child, Joybubbles found he could control the telephone network with whistles. The dialing system converts numbers into sound tones, which command the telephone exchanges to direct the call. Joybubbles became the first "phreaker," a hacker who takes control of phone systems—and makes free calls—by using whistles. (It doesn't work anymore.)

1967 INSIDE IBM

In 1967, IBM donated four computer terminals to a high school near Chicago. Each terminal was connected to a mainframe at IBM's offices. IBM set up some space on the mainframe for the students to use, keeping them separate from other users. Students soon worked out how to hack into private areas of the network. IBM eventually thanked the kids, because their hack helped IBM make their systems more secure.

1971 CAPTAIN CRUNCH

John Draper, also known as Captain Crunch, discovered that a toy whistle he got as a free gift in a box of Cap'n Crunch cereal made just the right tone to access long-distance phone calls for free. Draper was threatened with prison if he did not stop hacking. He later met Steve Jobs and Steve Wozniak, two students who made and sold phreaking devices—and then later set up the computer company Apple.

1981 CAPTAIN ZAP

Ian Murphy, better known as Captain Zap, claimed to have carried out the greatest hack ever. He hacked into the largest telephone provider in the United States and changed the system's internal clock so that people who used the phone at peak times during the day were charged at cheaper night-time rates.

WHAT'S WHAT?

WARGAMES

The first time many people heard about hacking—and the Internet—was in the 1983 film *WarGames*. It's about a pair of teenagers who hack a government computer and take control of nuclear weapons. They use an early hacking technique called "war dialing" where their computer dials different numbers until it connects to another computer.

WHO'S WHO?

THE 414S

The 414s were a real-life teenage hacking group, six boys from Milwaukee, Wisconsin. In the early 1980s, few organizations used complex passwords, so the 414s easily hacked banks, hospitals, and the US government labs where nuclear weapons had been invented. In response, the United States government wrote new laws to discourage others from copying them.

1984 CHAOS COMMUNICATIONS CONGRESS

The first "hackercon," or meeting of hackers, was held in Hamburg, Germany, in 1984 and has been held every year since. It is run by the Chaos Computer Club, a German-language hacking association with more than 7,000 members.

1988 MORRIS WORM

Robert Morris spread a worm that shut down 10 percent of the network that is now called the Internet. In those days, that meant attacking just 6,000 computers. Even so, Morris's stunt caused $15 million in damages and he lost his job at Cornell University. In response, the US government set up CERT (Computer Emergency Response Team) to protect against similar computer attacks.

WILL FUTURE TECHNOLOGY BE HACK PROOF?

The history of hacking is about people taking advantage of weaknesses in a system to play pranks or cause damage. Everyone else is unaware of the system's flaws until they've been hacked. As we keep developing new technology, how can we trust that there aren't flaws in these systems for hackers to take advantage of? Should we be more wary?

HELLO INTERNET

The Internet is a network of computers. More correctly it is an "internetwork" that connects many separate computer networks. Exactly what that means has become blurred in the 50 years that the Internet has existed. The Internet connects billions of devices—several for every person on the planet—not just computers, phones, and tablets, but TVs, cars, weather stations, lamp posts, fridges, and ovens. And all these devices could be hacked.

192.968.0.0

MILITARY PROJECT

The Internet began as a military defense project. By the 1960s, military commanders were developing systems that relied on computers and telecommunications to control their forces. The military realized that the enemy could gain a huge advantage if they were able to sever these communications—and to do that they just needed to cut one cable. The ARPANET (Advanced Research Projects Agency Network) was set up to keep communications safe even during the worst attacks.

PACKET SWITCHING

ARPANET used a system called "packet switching," in which a message is broken into chunks or "packets." Each packet has a header code which says where it's from, where it's going, and how it fits together with the other packets. Each packet makes its own way to its destination through the network. The receiving computer assembles the packets and sends back a message requesting any missing packets to be resent. This is how everything from videos to text messages are sent through the Internet today.

The rules that control how data moves through the Internet are called the Internet **Protocol**. Every connection to the Internet has an identity number called its IP address.

One of the things ARPANET did was to send electronic mail, or email. Messages like these had been whizzing around computer networks for most of the 1960s, going from one named user to another. But as the number of users grew, a new, more precise system was needed. Computer scientist Ray Tomlinson added a "domain" to the address—name@mycomputer—the part after @ showed where on the network a particular person was.

SWITCH ON

ARPANET was switched on in 1969. At first, it connected just four US universities, mostly in California, but it steadily spread and, by 1973, other countries were connected. In the 1980s, the military built a separate system, and ARPANET was connected to the telephone networks used by the public. By the late 1980s it had become known as the Internet.

COMPUTER SIGNS

The @ (at), * (star), and # (hash) symbols get a lot of use on the Internet. **The @ symbol predates email**. It is at least 500 years old and was first used as a symbol for the Spanish weight "arroba." This word comes from the Arabic for quarter (عبرلا), and @ might be a mash up of the letter "a" and ‹بع›.

The proper name for * is asterisk. It can be used to represent unknown characters in a web search. It dates from ancient Greece, 2,200 years ago, and was originally used to signal additional text at the bottom of a page.

The #—used for hashtags—is called the octothorpe. It appears in print as far back as 1850 and probably evolved from a quick way of writing "lb," the symbol for a pound weight. In the United States, # is still called the pound sign.

THE WEB

In the early days, the Internet was all about File Transfer Protocol , the "FTP," used for sending and receiving computer files quickly and securely. However, in 1989, Tim Berners-Lee, a British computer scientist working at CERN (the European Organisation for Nuclear Research), found the system hard to use. He came up with the idea of a web of information—a world-wide web—where users could look at publicly available files on an Internet-connected computer.

In 1990, Berners-Lee created a piece of software called a "web browser" which showed a user the "web page" of another computer. This listed the files that were available to view—things like documents, data, and pictures. When you use the World Wide Web, your browser acts as a window for looking into another computer.

WYSIWYG GUI

The rise of the Web went hand in hand with the GUI (goo-ee)—the "graphical user interface." Instead of blinking green text on a black screen, users now had a virtual desktop, with files and documents that could be opened and moved around. Users used to control a computer by typing code, but now they clicked onscreen graphics using a mouse. The GUI made it possible for computing to be WYSIWYG (wiz-ee-wig), or "what you see is what you get." So a typed document appeared on screen as a white page with printed text and pictures—just like the real thing.

HYPERLINKS

Berners-Lee's World Wide Web of information could link one web page to the next with clickable "hyperlinks." Documents with a hyperlink are written in HTML (hypertext mark-up language), again developed by Berners-Lee, but the idea for hyperlinks was the brainchild of Vannevar Bush, a computer pioneer in the 1940s. Some 1980s software applications used links, but Berners-Lee's idea to connect the links through the Internet changed history—and we've been surfing the Web ever since.

WHAT'S WHAT?

HTTP://

Every item on the Web has a "uniform resource locater" or URL, better known as a web address. The first web address ever is *http://info.cern.ch/hypertext/WWW/TheProject*. Http stands for Hypertext Transfer Protocol, the set of rules that manages web traffic through the net.

WHO OWNS THE INTERNET?

All the content on the Web belongs to someone, somewhere, probably the person who produced it or paid for it to be made. Computers throughout the world all have an owner, as do the cables and **infrastructure** that join them together. Do the owners of the infrastructure own the Internet? Or is it everyone's?

MAKING CONNECTIONS

Time to get better acquainted with your computer hardware, and begin to see it like a hacker does: a series of devices that provide a connection to your computer and your information. A computer is composed of **hardware** and **software**. The hardware is the physical stuff. The software is the invisible instructions that tell the hardware what to do. A hacker knows how to take control of the hardware or software.

YOU AND THE CPU

A computer receives an **input** from you, the user. It uses the instructions in its software programming to convert that input into an output. For example, pressing the "H" key on the keyboard results in an :h" appearing on the screen. The CPU, or central processing unit, is the chunky microchip "brain" that does this work. Everything else in the hardware setup is there to give the CPU what it needs to do its job.

The other crucial internal hardware is the RAM, or random access memory. This is a temporary holding position for the CPU to keep important data while it is thinking about something else. The more RAM a computer has, the easier it will be for the CPU to do its job quickly.

The content you create on a computer needs to be stored. You might just save it on the computer's hard drive, which records digital files as magnetied patterns on a metal disk. Tablets, phones, and little laptops store files on microchips. You can store files on CDs, DVDs, external drives, and of course there is "The Cloud," which is really just a big storage computer that you connect to via the Internet. Where does the Internet fit in to all this? Turn the page to find out.

Turn the page to find out.

MODEM

A modem or modulator-demodulator is the device that transfers data between your computer and the Internet. The first modems turned outputs from a computer into sound signals that traveled along telephone wires. A modem at the other end converted the sounds back into data. Today, modems receive pure digital data sent along a cable.

INPUT HARDWARE

These are the devices that collect inputs from the user. The most obvious ones are the keyboard, mouse, and touchscreen, which convert the pressure of your fingertips into commands that the CPU can understand. Other inputs come from a camera or scanner, which create digital versions of a physical object, and increasingly we are controlling our devices via sound inputs picked up by a microphone.

OUTPUTS

After the CPU has done its job, it will present an **output** to another piece of hardware. The one we all think of first is the computer display, or monitor, which shows the text, pictures, video, or whatever we want from our device. A loudspeaker allows for sonic outputs—you might call that music (but Grandad will disagree). Meanwhile, a printer produces a hard copy of what's on screen, or perhaps a solid 3D version.

NET CONNECT

The Internet can do everything: it is an input (a streamed video of cats from Gran), an output (an email thanking Gran), and storage (pictures of Gran's cat stored on the Cloud). This is what makes the Internet so amazingly useful and why it has transformed society. However, that great power comes with big risks. How can your computer be wide open to what the Internet offers but be secure at the same time?

GOING WIRELESS

Today most Internet connections are wireless, and there are two main types. WiFi is a radio connection with a modem somewhere nearby. The technology is super smart. It can work out whose signal is whose among a jumble of radio waves. The second wireless connection is mobile internet (such as 3G or 4G). Your phone works like a walkie-talkie, exchanging radio signals with a nearby mobile tower, which is hardwired to the Internet.

The WiFi network in a home, school, or office is part of a LAN or local area network . Each device connected to the LAN can talk to each other, and they all share the same connection to the Internet (which could be described as a WAN, or wide area network). That connection is protected by a firewall, which is a software filter that prevents hackers from outside connecting to the LAN.

A VPN, or virtual private network, is a service where any connection you make—through any modem or mobile tower—works as if you are connecting to a private network instead of the public Internet. All traffic into and out of your device is encrypted. As well as protecting your communications, a VPN is also a means of hiding the location of your device and what you are doing with it, so you can be sure hackers are using VPNs too.

WHO'S WHO?

HARALD BLUETOOTH

When you connect two devices to share pictures or transfer money, you are using a short range radio connection called Bluetooth. This system is named after Harald Bluetooth, a 10th-century Viking king who first unified Denmark into one country. Bluetooth tech was so-named because it allows computers and phones to unify into one.

SECRETS IN PUBLIC

Out in the Internet, your communications are public. This is where encryption is required. Let's say you want to buy something online. If your payment details were public, a hacker could use them to buy stuff for themselves—only you'd pay. Your payment details are encrypted, or made secret, using a numerical padlock which would take the world's biggest computers thousands of years to decode. Even if a hacker was watching the whole thing, your secret is very safe indeed.

WHO KEEPS YOUR COMPUTER SECURE?

So now you know more about what is coming into and out of your computer and how it makes connections. Whose job is it to keep your computer safe from attack? The manufacturer? Your phone and Internet provider? The websites you use? Or is it all down to you?

HACKING TECHNIQUES

Hackers are computer nerds and confidence tricksters rolled into one. Some hack attacks are high-tech actions that use in-depth knowledge of the software that controls computers and the Internet. Other hacks prey on the way people think to play tricks on them. The simplest hack of all is to just ask someone for their passwords! However, most hacking techniques are a mixture of software skills and social trickery, and hackers like to give them weird names. Let's take a look.

Not all malware needs a person to spread it (knowingly or not). A computer worm uses the software that manages networks to make and distribute copies of itself. A worm that is good at this will multiply over and over and eventually stop the network from functioning. An anti-worm is a worm that is produced to do good things. For example, they can find and destroy software infected with viruses or upgrade old security systems to a safer setup.

MALWARE

The sneakiest way of hacking your system is to add malware, or malicious software. Malware might automatically damage your files or it might create a "back door," through which a hacker can secretly take control of the computer. The most familiar malware is the virus, which the user installs on their device without realizing and which spreads from one computer to another, often as email attachments. Another user opens the attachment—and the virus has found a new victim.

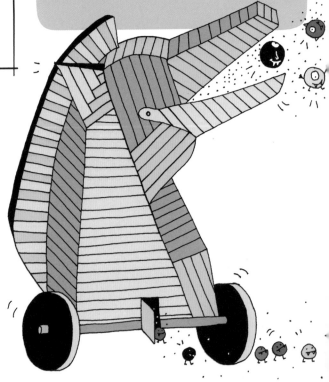

TROJAN HORSE

Just as in the myth about Greek soldiers hiding in a giant horse to get past the guards outside the city of Troy, a hacker uses a software "Trojan" to install malware. It looks like a harmless app or attachment, but once launched, a Trojan installs secret malware. Keeping your software up to date is the best defense against malware because it stops hackers from taking advantage of flaws in the code.

WHO'S WHO?

THE GRANDADDY OF VIRUSES

Just two years after the Internet was turned on in 1969, the first computer virus began to spread through it. It was written by Ray Tomlinson, the computer scientist who also invented email. The virus didn't damage infected computers, but simply printed out a message: "I'm the Creeper: Catch me if you can."

WHAT'S WHAT?

THE LOVE BUG

The most damaging malware in history was the Love Bug. It arrived in a file called ILOVEYOU. Over ten days in May 2000, 50 million people opened the file, releasing a worm, which sent 50 copies to other people before wiping files and crashing the computer. By May 15th, a tenth of the Internet was infected and it cost $8 billion to fix!

Trojans are a common way of delivering ransomware. This very nasty software prevents a user from accessing the computer. All they can see on the screen is a threat to wipe the computer's hard disk unless they pay a large amount of money.

SOCIAL ENGINEERING

Another way of hacking a computer is described as "social engineering." Here's how it might happen. The phone rings and a voice says, "Hi, I'm from the IT department, there is a problem with your computer. I need your password so I can log in from here and fix it." Sounds reasonable enough, but don't be fooled. Hackers use a range of tricks to convince us to give away secrets or grant them access to our devices.

Connecting to the Internet is pretty essential for our devices to work properly, and that is a weakness hackers exploit. Just as lions wait at a waterhole for prey to come for a drink, a hacker lures in victims with the promise of free WiFi. Once you connect, the hacker can see all the messages coming in and out of your device, read your emails, collect passwords, and even install malware in secret.

PHISHING

This dangerous social hack hooks you by sending a message that seems to come from a service that you use, such as a bank. The message asks you to log in to your account, but the link provided takes you to a fake webpage. You type in your security details and you get an error message asking you to try again later. But the hacker now has all the security details they need to login to your accounts for real!

CRACKING PASSWORDS

If a hacker cannot trick you out of your password or guess it, they will use a "brute force attack" by trying every possible sequence of characters. Adding more characters to your password, such as upper and lower case letters and numbers, increases the number of possible permutations.

Possible passwords with 8 characters

lowercase letters:	208,827,064,576
upper and lowercase letters:	53,459,728,531,456
letters and numbers:	218,340,105,584,896
including special characters:	6,634,204,312,890,625

A hacker might repurpose a graphics unit from a gaming console or use hundreds of computers at once, which could crack an 8-character lowercase password in 1.8 seconds. So, how safe is your password?

CLICKJACKING

A "clickjacking" attack tricks the user into clicking on a hidden web link. The hacker does this by setting up a very appealing website, such as one that supplies downloads of pirated movies. However, the links on the screen are fake, and when a user clicks on one, they are actually selecting another invisible link. A hacker could use this trick to steal passwords and other details saved by an Internet browser.

If a hacker could access your keyboard just imagine what they could learn. The most common method for this is to use a piece of malware called a keylogger, which simply records every key you press in order—including all your passwords. Expert hackers (and government spies) are said to be able to analyze the sound of typing to figure out a password.

ZOMBIES AND BOTNETS

Once a hacker has found a way into your computer, he or she can turn it into a "zombie." The hacker then puts the zombie's processor and RAM to work in secret. The user has no indication of this, apart from their device running slowly on occasion. Hackers assemble armies of zombie computers into "botnets." Working together, a botnet of thousands of zombies is as powerful as a supercomputer.

ROOTKIT

Probably the worst hack attack is the "rootkit." This malware inserts itself into a computer's most fundamental software, the operating system, which manages how all the components work together. The rootkit's job is to hide other malware. Any security software designed to search for and clean out malware relies on the operating system. However, as the rootkit is hidden in there, it can disguise other malware as legitimate bits of software.

A "logic bomb" is a feature of malware designed to act when a particular set of conditions are met. In 2006, Roger Duronio had bet against the value of the bank he worked for. He planned to disrupt its computer network with a logic bomb just before the stock market opened. News of the problem would make everyone withdraw their money from the bank, he thought, and the share price would tumble. The plan failed, and Duronio went to prison.

A common use of a botnet is a "denial of service," or DoS, attack. A hacker uses this technique to bring down a target website. The botnet's zombie computers are instructed to send out a stream of requests to view the website. The computer, or computers, hosting the website crash because they cannot handle all that traffic. DoS attacks are tricky to defend against because the requests flood in from all over the world.

A HONEYPOT

The good guys can be sneaky too. A "honeypot" is a cyber-security term for a computer that has been set up to look like a weak point in a larger network. When hackers try to get in through the honeypot, the real network is completely safe, and the bad guys are caught red handed.

WHAT'S WHAT?

SKIMMING

Hackers can use technology to steal money right out of your pocket. Contactless credit cards pay for things by sending a signal to a card reader. The card has a tag inside, which becomes electrified when a powerful radio source is nearby—an inch of so normally. Once electrified, the tag sends out a unique signal, which identifies it to the reader. A "skimmer" uses a card reader in crowds to steal cash by collecting these signals. Mobile phone payment apps also work in this way, only the phone demands a signal back from the reader to boost security.

WHEN DOES HACKING BECOME ILLEGAL?

Let's assume that someone who hacks your stuff is doing it to steal money or identity details. That activity is obviously a crime. But at what point does the hacker cross the line? Is it only when they actually steal from you, or is it when they use deception, take control of your computer, or stop or limit your use of it?

HACKER CULTURE

Hackers sound like scary people; their skills let them attack and take over your devices to steal whatever they want without ever leaving their homes. Hackers are generally antisocial. They prefer to spend time with computers than with other people, but they are not universally a bad bunch. Let's take a closer look at how hackers see themselves.

CRACKER
The criminal hacker that gives the rest of them a bad name, intent on breaking in wherever they are not wanted to steal secrets and wreak havoc.

SCRIPT KIDDIE
A wannabe cracker who lacks skills and causes trouble using "scripts" (code and apps) developed by others and widely available on the web.

PHREAKER
An expert in attacking the security of telephone systems and networks in general.

CYPHERPUNK
A person whose main interest is cracking encryption.

WARES DOODZ
A hacker who specializes in making illegal copies of **copyrighted** software and distributing it—for free or for sale. The software may be a Trojan.

IRONMONGER
A hardware specialist who works in the manufacture and maintenance of motherboards, memory, and processors— and so is looked down upon by hackers (see also Sandbender).

SNEAKER
A hacker who's hired by a company or organization to test its cyber defenses by trying to break in from the outside. A group of sneakers is a "tiger team."

ALPHA GEEK

The most skilled and experienced member of a hacking collective, to whom other members will turn for help.

CHOMPER

A failed hacker whose attempts at hacking are ineffectual; also called a "luser" (a mashup of loser and user).

CODE GRINDER

An IT professional who has no interest in hacking. Hackers feel sorry for them.

JOCK

A hacker whose main technique is to use brute force attacks to break through security.

HIRED GUN

A hacker employed by a criminal gang to provide programming services as part of a wider conspiracy. Similar to a "samurai," who is employed to provide the same service on a legal basis.

SANDBENDER

An electronics engineer who designs and manufactures silicon microchips, a role that does not appeal to hackers because it requires patience, precision, and teamwork. (The most common source of silicon in the world is sand.)

UBERGEEK

A hacker—generally a wizard (see below)—who has made an impact on the wider community, especially for writing programs that are in common use by others.

LEECH

A particular kind of luser who downloads shared files but does not make them available to others.

WIZARD

A hacker with expert knowledge of one particular piece of hardware or software that far exceeds the abilities of a general hacker.

HACKER ETHIC

Don't assume hacking is always a malicious activity designed to cheat and steal. A hack arises from repurposing a technology for another use, improving older techniques by merging new ideas, and, when necessary, fixing a problem with whatever is at hand at the time. To achieve this, hackers live by a set of rules called the "hacker **ethic**," and these values can be at odds with the way society at large views things:

Information is free. A hacker needs to have access to everything anyone knows. That leads to better hacks. But what about personal secrets?

All computer technology should be available to everyone, not just the people who devise and own it. Hackers want to take it apart to see how it all works—and figure out how to hack it. They believe this can only be of benefit to society as a whole, but the owners of the technology may lose out.

Hackers do not want any authority to interfere with them because the best results come when people work alone and collaborate when they choose to. But how does a system like this prevent bad behavior?

A hacker is only judged by the quality of their hacks, not by any qualifications and certainly not by race, gender, or creed. But is it possible to judge the skill of a hack without considering its consequences?

WHAT'S WHAT?

SILICON VALLEY

Until the 1970s, Silicon Valley, a region south of San Francisco, California, was called the Santa Clara Valley. William Shockley was one of the inventors of the transistor, an electronic device used in today's microchips. This work was done in New Jersey, but in the early 1950s, Shockley set up a transistor factory near his ailing mother, who lived in the Santa Clara Valley. Before long, the area was packed with computer companies—and hackers.

HOMEBREW COMPUTER CLUB

Today's hacker culture took a lot from a group called the Homebrew Computer Club who met in Silicon Valley in the early 1970s. Being from Silicon Valley, they had access to all the latest developments in computer technology. Many members went on to have stellar careers in computing: Adam Osborne designed the first portable laptops; Steve Wozniak was one of the founders of Apple; Dan Werthimer set up SETI, the Search for Extraterrestrial **Intelligence**; while Jerry Lawson pioneered home gaming consoles.

Have you heard of **life hacks**? These are shortcuts or new techniques that make life easier. There are thousands on YouTube of varying usefulness, ranging from pranks to clever fixes for everyday problems. They are hacks nevertheless because they use common pre-existing technologies rather than a new invention or product.

? IS HACKING CULTURE COOL?

So now you know a little more about who hackers are as people and as a group. Do you admire them? Do you like the idea of being one of them? What is so fascinating about hackers? What is it that makes them cool?

BLACK HATS AND WHITE HATS

The online world is sometimes compared to the days of the Wild West in the United States, where cowboys and gunslingers did what they wanted and were rarely brought to justice. In classic Western movies of the 1950s and 60s, it was simple to figure out who was good and who was bad because the good guys always wore white hats, while the baddies donned black hats. Hackers are often described in the same way.

BLACK HAT

As you might expect, a "black hat" is a criminal cracker who breaks through security for nefarious reasons. Some notorious black hats include:

David Smith (USA) who unleashed the Melissa virus in 1999, which infected email applications all over the world at an estimated cost of $80 million.

Jeanson Ancheta (USA) who was sent to prison for five years after he was found to be in control of a botnet of over 100,000 zombie computers in 2006.

Hamza Bendelladj (Algeria) who infected 50 million computers with viruses and stole $400 million from banks (and donated it to charity). Bendelladj was sentenced to 15 years in prison.

White hats come in teams. A red team will attack from the outside while an opposing team of experts—the blue team—will defend from inside the network.

Copyright ensures that anything someone produces belongs to them, and no one can copy it without permission. Richard Stallman proposed the concept of "copyleft," which works the opposite way. Copyleft means that everything is free to share and modify, but every new version created from it is also free to share.

WHITE HAT

"White hats" know all the tricks and techniques to break through cybersecurity but do not use them for criminal purposes. An organization employs a white hat to help them improve their security and keep black hats out. Often the white hat works as a "sneaker," an operative who has permission to break into an organization's network—or at least try—but few people at the organization know in advance that they are about to be attacked.

WHO'S WHO?

RICHARD STALLMAN

Richard Stallman, a hacker since the early 1970s, probably came up with the terms "black hat" and "white hat." Stallman is very much a white hat himself. He is best known for developing entirely free software through the GNU Project. GNU stands for GNU's Not Unix—Stallman wants you to go around in circles on that one. Unix is an operating system, and in 1991, Stallman and hundreds of GNU collaborators released Linux, a free alternative operating system.

WHAT'S WHAT?

GRAY HAT

A "gray hat" is a hacker who looks for flaws in software. If they find anything, they share the discovery with the people concerned and ask for a reward. If no reward is given, then the gray hat exploits the flaw in some way, perhaps making it public to embarrass the owners.

IS IT OK FOR BLACK HATS TO BECOME WHITE?

Black hat hackers get caught in the end. The police have a lot of money and resources—including the best white hats—devoted to tracking them down. Once a black hat has been punished, is it okay to ask them to be a white hat? They are obviously experts and could be well paid to protect us from other black hats. Is that fair?

HACKTIVISM

Hacking can be used as a force for change. When hackers are also political **activists**, they become "hacktivists." A hacktivist uses their technology skills to apply political pressure by carrying out an online protest. As you can imagine, hacktivism is a morally difficult area, and some people who see themselves as politically motivated freedom fighters are regarded as spies and even terrorists by others.

CULT OF THE DEAD COW

The story of hacktivism begins in a disused slaughterhouse in Lubbock, Texas, in 1984. Here, three friends formed the Cult of the Dead Cow (or cDc), coordinating a wider team of hackers via bulletin boards (a pre-Web message system—see page 56.) In the late 1990s, the cDc launched the Hacktivismo group, which combated censorship on the Web and created tools for use by political dissidents around the world.

ANONYMOUS

The most famous hacktivist group is Anonymous. It has no leader and is made up of people from all over the world, who communicate via online forums using usernames or "handles." Once Anonymous members—the Anons—agree on a target, they work alone or in small teams and their actions accumulate into a coherent attack. Anonymous generally blocks a target's communications and tries to access secret information to highlight what the Anons perceive as wrongdoing.

It was a different world back in 2003, when **Anonymous** began. So different that people still used fax machines. A fax is a printer-scanner that copies a sheet of paper and sends it down a phone line to another fax, which prints it out. An early hacktivist technique was the black fax: a loop of black paper was fed through a machine, making the target fax print black sheets until it ran out of paper— thus rendering it useless.

WHAT'S WHAT?

V FOR VENDETTA

Anonymous also carry out real-life protests organized by Twitter accounts—anonymous ones. It has become the tradition that Anonymous protesters stay anonymous by wearing a Guy Fawkes mask as worn by the fictional hacktivist V, from a 1982 comic series called *V for Vendetta*. The story was made into a film in 2006, around the time the Anonymous group was growing in stature, and Anons began sharing images of the mask online.

LULZSEC

With a name that means "laughing at security" in hacker-speak, LulzSec were not interested in making money, but sought revenge against companies that they thought needed to be taught a lesson. They targeted media companies, political parties, and even cybersecurity firms. One of their more effective pranks was to reroute their enemy's customer service telephone lines to different companies. The seven ringleaders of LulzSec —none of whom had ever met—were arrested in 2012. The youngest was just 16.

Sony was famously hacked in 2014 when an entire movie, and more, was stolen. The unknown hackers, who people suspect were working for North Korea, insisted that Sony did not release a comedy film called *The Interview*, which made fun of North Korea's leader Kim Jong-un, including showing him be assassinated in a funny way. In the end, Sony released the film online for free.

WIKILEAKS

The most notorious hacktivist group is Wikileaks. It was founded in 2006 by Julian Assange, an Australian with an extensive hacking past. Wikileaks styles itself as a new kind of media platform. It receives information from whistleblowers, or people who reveal the secrets of a government or organization to highlight what they believe to be wrongdoing. Wikileaks then releases this information—or at least some of it—often in collaboration with newspapers around the world.

THE LEAKS

Here are some of the biggest wiki-leaks in recent years:

July 2010, Collateral murder: The cockpit video from a US Army helicopter showed a minibus of journalists being machine-gunned by mistake.

November 2010, Diplomatic cables: A quarter of a million messages (or cables) sent by US diplomats over nearly 50 years were published. The messages contained gossip about world leaders plus some top secret information. A US soldier, Chelsea Manning, admitted leaking the information and went to prison.

July, 2016, Democratic National Committee emails: 20,000 emails sent by members of the US Democratic Party during the 2016 US presidential election were released. The emails made people lose trust in Hillary Clinton, and her opponent Donald Trump won the election. The US intelligence services said that the hackers who stole the emails and gave them to Wikileaks were probably working for the Russian government.

A WANTED MAN

In 2010, Julian Assange was asked to go to Sweden for questioning over sexual assaults. He refused and in 2012, went to live inside the Ecuadorian Embassy in London. He was given Ecuadorian citizenship, which meant that he could not be arrested if he stayed inside. In 2019 Ecuador took away his citizenship, and so the British police arrested him and sent him to prison. Assange is still wanted in Sweden, and the United States has also accused him of hacking their secrets.

Wikileaks guarantees the anonymity of its sources. Leakers leave information in a drop box built and maintained by Assange and others. Even Wikileaks cannot know who provided the information, and so they can never be forced to tell the authorities. Your secret is safe with them.

WIKILEAKS
DROP BOX

WHO'S WHO?

JULIAN ASSANGE

In the late 1980s and early 1990s, Assange was a well-known hacker who made attacks on NASA, **the Pentagon**, and the US Navy. Wikileaks grew slowly at first but was world famous by 2010. Assange's style of journalism made him enemies in many governments, because he published secrets that other news outlets would not.

WHAT'S WHAT?

WIKI WHAT?

In the language of the World Wide Web, a "wiki" is a website that can be edited by anyone. The most famous wiki is Wikipedia, the world's largest website, which has articles on just about anything all created by volunteer writers and editors around the world. Wikileaks is a catchy name but it is not actually a wiki.

? CAN EVERYONE KEEP SECRETS?

A person has the right to keep secrets and keep their life private. We can all agree on that, but does a government have the same right to secrecy? They work for us, so why aren't we allowed to know certain things? Are there any good reasons for this kind of secrecy?

CULTURE JAMMING

Here's an idea. Print the old social media posts of politicians on huge posters, stick them up on billboards, and *then* post photos of it on social media. Everyone takes more notice of what the politicians said. This is "culture jamming," also known as "reality hacking" or "guerrilla communications," and it's where hacking meets the real world.

FLASHMOB

When a crowd of strangers suddenly transforms into a group who all start to do the same things—dancing, singing, or standing completely still—that's a flashmob. As suddenly as it started, the flashmob is over, and the participants disappear back into the crowd. The first flashmob was in New York City in 2003, when 130 people went to a department store and suddenly asked to buy the same rug all at the same time!

SHARING MEMES

The original concept of a meme was a thought experiment by biologist Richard Dawkins. He wanted to explore how simple ideas, which he called memes, spread through a process like biological evolution, moving from person to person, changing or mutating as they go. The Internet makes sharing ideas very easy, and so the term "meme" generally now applies to something fun that has spread via the Web.

MEMORABLE MEMES

Here are some of the more popular memes to take over the internet.

Rickrolling: When a link to a piece of appealing content turns out to be a clip of *Never Gonna Give You Up*, a song by Rick Astley from the 1980s.

Planking: People share photos of themselves lying face down in the most incongruous places.

Mannequin Challenge: A group of people stand perfectly still during a video as if they were mannequins.

SUBVERTISING

The most visible form of culture jamming is "subvertising," which subverts advertising to change the message. The usual method is to alter the word by removing or changing letters. This technique dates back to the 1950s but today it is much easier to digitally alter familiar ads and share them online.

In the summer of 2005, 21-year-old Alex Tew set up *http://www.milliondollarhomepage.com/* Apart from a banner across the top, the page was a blank black page made up of 1 million black pixels. Tew said each pixel was for sale at $1 each, and the new owners could put pictures and links on their pixels. Word soon spread and within five months Tew had made $1 million.

FOR ART OR FOR PROFIT?

Culture jamming has been used as a fun form of art or for making protests that try to change the way people think about stuff. Now culture jams are used to sell us things. Is that ok or does that spell the end of this kind of hack?

ESPIONAGE AND SURVEILLANCE

When does a hacker become a spy or a spy become a hacker? A determined hacker might creep inside a high-security compound to install malware to gain access to a target's information. A spy might do exactly the same thing. The only real difference is that hackers are generally criminals, while spies are hired to do it, by a government or organization. Let's explore the spooky world of espionage.

SOURCES OF INFORMATION

In the language of espionage, any information that helps you understand your target better is called intelligence. The most obvious way to gather intelligence is when someone from a foreign power or an enemy group changes side ("defects" is the spy term) and tells what they know. As well as this human intelligence, the world's spies are increasingly relying on signals intelligence—intercepting messages and working out what they mean. Sounds like a job for a hacker.

SIDE-CHANNEL ATTACKS

The United States and the United Kingdom, both use a "side-channel attack" system called TEMPEST to pick up signals that leak from their targets. This works out the content of a message not by collecting the coded data itself, but by watching how the computer and its user behave. The message itself is hidden, but the sounds, vibrations, radio waves, and other electrical echoes given out by the computer system may give away secrets.

SURVEILLANCE

Not the same as spying, **surveillance** is the practice of watching general activity. Police might use it to watch for crimes and track the movements of wanted individuals. Cameras (sometimes called **CCTV**) are a major tool, with many able to read car registration plates via ANPR or automated number-plate recognition. However, CCTV is seldom of good enough quality to track targets using automated facial recognition—not yet anyway.

It is not just spies who are becoming hackers—businesspeople are doing it too! Most trading on stock markets is managed by algorithms. These systems, called algos, respond to tiny shifts in prices and buy and sell items in a fraction of a second. An algo's job is also to hide what a trader plans to do—so rivals cannot do it first. Traders also have algo-sniffers, which search through market activity to spot an algo at work.

WHO'S WHO?

FIVE EYES

This is the world's most powerful intelligence alliance, made up of the major English speaking powers: the United States, Canada, New Zealand, Australia, and the United Kingdom. The five members share their intelligence, and in some cases are asked to spy on each other's populations to get around internal laws.

WHAT'S WHAT?

SPYWARE

Malware used to spy on people is called spyware. We have come across this already with the keylogger, which records whatever is being typed. Similar spyware detects mouse clicks or impressions on a touchscreen. Another common target of spyware—by hackers as well as professional spies—are webcams, which can be switched on remotely.

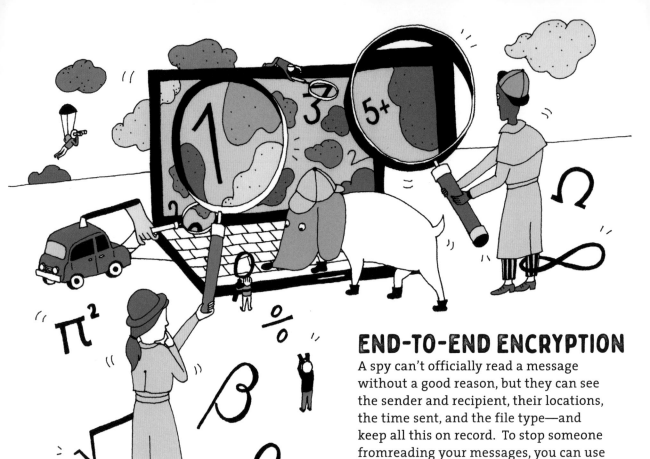

END-TO-END ENCRYPTION

A spy can't officially read a message without a good reason, but they can see the sender and recipient, their locations, the time sent, and the file type—and keep all this on record. To stop someone fromreading your messages, you can use end-to-end encryption messaging apps. All your chat threads will be encrypted from your device to the recipient. Not even the app provider can read them.

BULK INTERCEPTION

Spies want to know as much as they can about their targets, and that means searching for enemy agents hiding out among the public. To do that, spy agencies have increasingly started to watch everyone, looking for clues as to where the bad guys are. This does not mean studying CCTV of the street, it means collecting information about everyone's communications and filtering them to reveal secret messages sent by criminals, terrorists, and enemy spies.

Police and spy agencies have asked their governments to be given access to end-to-end encryptions. There may be a very good reason, such as wanting to see messages from a terrorist to prevent a new attack. However, if encryption was weakened by an official back door which would let the authorities read hidden messages, it would only be a matter of time before hackers—the bad kind—would find a way in.

WATCHING THE WATCHERS

A surveillance camera can't see everything and its footage might give the wrong impression about an event. Some private citizens carry their own cameras to record more accurate accounts of a situation. For example, cyclists wear helmet cameras in case they get into an accident. This is "sousveillance." It means to watch from underneath (*sous* means "below" in French).

Many countries have a freedom of information law to balance out the powers of state to collect information about people. Anybody is allowed to request to see the information recorded about them by the state—and that includes any images on CCTV. However, intelligence services are allowed to keep their work secret.

WHO'S WHO?

FARADAY CAGE

To stay completely out of sight of the authorities, your computer needs to be "air gapped"—or not connected to any public network. You'll also need a "Faraday cage," named after Michael Faraday who developed early electrical technology. This metal cage surrounds your computer and acts as a shield for any electrical signal coming in or going out. The world's best spies could be outside trying to listen in, but they won't get a thing.

WHAT'S WHAT?

THE PANOPTICON

The 18th-century English philosopher Jeremy Bentham had an idea of the perfect prison, which he called the Panopticon. A single guard could watch every prisoner at the same time using a system of mirrors. The idea was that prisoners would behave themselves because they thought they were being watched all the time.

HOW MUCH PRIVACY DO WE NEED?

It is often said that if you have done nothing wrong, you have nothing to hide. Is a peaceful, happy society one where everyone is watched? Why does anyone have a right to privacy?

THE WHISTLEBLOWER

In June 2013, American intelligence official Edward Snowden told the world what the spying agencies in his country and others were doing. As a computer expert, Snowden knew many techniques used by intelligence agencies to hack into foreign communication systems and listen in to just about any conversation in the world.

To escape arrest in the United States, he moved to Moscow, Russia, where he still lives today.

Many of the spying programs outlined by Edward Snowden began following the 9/11 attacks on the United States in 2001. The intelligence services reasoned that they had missed the warning signs back then, and needed to be ready to counter future attacks. A few months after Snowden's leaks began, US lawmakers reviewed NSA's phone-tapping program and found it had not stopped any terror attacks so far. The NSA continues to argue that mass surveillance is essential.

SECRET PROGRAMS

Edward Snowden and a team of journalists revealed what the US National Security Agency (the NSA), UK Government Communications Head Quarters (GCHQ), and other similar agencies were capable of. These included:

PRISM: Most of the world's Internet traffic goes through the United States. The PRISM program allows the NSA to demand information about any internet user from Google, Facebook, Microsoft, and other large US companies.

Project Tempora: This allows GCHQ to temporarily store almost the entirety of Internet traffic by tapping the cables that connect Europe to North America.

XKeyscore: A program for searching through emails, text messages, and other communications of anyone whose data has been recorded by the PRISM and Tempora programs.

WHY DID HE DO IT?

Edward Snowden says he is a US patriot. The reason he "blew the whistle" was that he believed the US intelligence services had too much power. Even if the current intelligence system is working for the greater good today, Snowden questioned what would happen if that changed in the future and spying tools were used against ordinary people. He decided he needed to tell everyone what was going on so they could make up their own minds.

WHAT'S WHAT?

BLACK ROOMS

In 2006, a US telephone engineer, Mark Klein, revealed the function of Room 641A at an Internet exchange in San Francisco, which held a large number of fiber optic cables. Room 641A was one of many "black rooms" used by the intelligence services. Inside, the laser signals from the cables were being split in two—one beam continued on its intended journey, the other was recorded by the NSA.

641A

DOES THE GOVERNMENT KNOW TOO MUCH?

Opinion **polls** taken soon after Edward Snowden went public showed that about 45 percent of people believed the US was collecting too much surveillance data, while 40 percent thought the surveillance did not go far enough. Do you think Edward Snowden was right, or should he go to prison? Or do you think both these things at once?

WHOSE DATA IS IT?

Not only is our data at risk from hackers, the government is also collecting it—although almost certainly not reading it. However, there are other bodies out there who are very interested in our data. We are supplying information about ourselves all the time, about where we are, who we are with, what we spend money on, and what we think. To the Internet giants that kind of information is very valuable indeed.

THE COST OF FREE

Many of the services we use on the Internet are free. Searching the Web with Google, connecting with friends on Instagram, and watching videos on YouTube does not cost a penny. However, the companies that own these sites are some of the most profitable in the world. You pay for accessing these services not with money, but with your information. But you already knew that, didn't you? You definitely agreed to it when you signed up.

TARGETED ADVERTISING

Facebook, Google, and the other Internet giants make money from selling advertising. When you watch a TV show, the show is free to view, but the TV company gets money from companies who show you an ads for their product. On the Web though, advertisers use data to target their ads specifically at people who might be interested in their products. So while a TV company gets paid by one advertiser at a time, a Web company is getting income from thousands at once.

SOCIAL NETWORKS

Have you every wondered why social media sites ask to access the details of your contacts? It makes it easier for them to suggest friends for you to add to your network, but they are also interested in building a picture of who knows whom. It turns out that it is often a small world, with a small number of people, known as "hubs," who link everyone else together. Who's the hub in your social circle?

HEALTH APPS

It takes effort to live a healthy life in the modern world. Fitness trackers and health apps can measure how active we've been and, given the right data, the app can score our health and create fitness plans. Sounds good, but who else has this information? It would be very interesting to an employer or health insurance company. Health information is protected by strict privacy laws, and only you can give someone else access to it. Have you?

Some of the most interesting information about us is what we spend our money on. Banks, credit card companies and supermarkets have been collecting this kind of information for years. Online shops use this data to try to figure out what we will buy next and give us suggestions—perhaps even creating special offers just for us. Now we're saving even more money! Click, click!

WEB 2.0

At the start of the 21st century, the web began to change. Portals tried to keep hold of users by offering free content, such as news, video clips, games, and messaging services. The most successful services allowed users to create and share their own content in what became known as social media. Today, users spend much of their time online within social media sites such as YouTube and Facebook where their activities are monitored so they can be better targeted with advertising.

WEB 1.0

In the early days, way back in the 1990s, the World Wide Web was a collection of web pages made by companies and individuals, all hoping to get visitors to their "home page." There was much jostling among a new breed of Internet businesspeople to have their website be a "portal," the gateway through which users accessed the rest of the Web. The obvious contenders were search engines, which indexed the Web's content to help you find things.

Hackers and other computer enthusiasts formed the first online social networks in the 1980s through the bulletin board system. This predated the Web and allowed members to share messages and software. The best boards had tight-knit communities, even though they never met in person. Hackers used "elite boards." Members were heavily controlled to keep out police informants.

ONLINE PERSONA

Activity on social media is in many ways the same as life in public. You are responsible for what you say and do and everyone can see you do it. However, on social media you can adopt a persona that's different from your ordinary life. In this way activities on social media can become a performance to an audience, and online interactions can lack authenticity.

THE RIGHT TO BE FORGOTTEN

In many countries a person can request that information about them is removed from the Web or made unavailable in searches made in their own country. This right is welcomed by some as a way of removing malicious material, while others worry that it allows criminals to hide past deeds and for people to rewrite their own history.

COOKIES

Websites load software called cookies into your browser. These help the website recognize you, but can also be used to gather information about your other web activities. People have always been able to delete or block cookies, but a new set of laws called the General Data Protection Regulation (GDPR) means that sites must always ask permission to use them. You are asked to click "agree" every time you arrive at a new site—but you don't have to agree; that's up to you.

Psychographics is the search for patterns in the personal data collected by social media companies. For example, the data might suggest that people who like videos of cats also buy a lot of shoes and vote in the same way. Dividing people up into groups like this makes it easier to target ads and influence people in other ways. This kind of data analysis is in its early days and its effectiveness is disputed.

? IS IT A FAIR EXCHANGE?

Who owns the information about your activity on the Internet, especially in social media services that you access for free? Is that data yours or does it belong to the service provider? If the data is yours, you must give it away in return for accessing social media. Is it worth it?

NET NEUTRALITY

Once information enters the Internet, it becomes just one more packet of data. Your email hasn't arrived? That's because it's waiting its turn to be routed through the network along with instant messages, photo uploads, and podcast downloads. It will arrive soon enough. But what if you could pay extra so all your data got to skip the line. In fact, why can't you do that already?

NET NEUTRALITY

The Internet isn't free. Someone somewhere is paying to connect your devices to the Web, even at the cafe with "free" WiFi. A company that offers Web access is called an Internet Service Provider or ISP. In most countries, your ISP must allow all customers the same access to the Internet, whatever they're using the connection for—be it streaming a movie or videoconferencing a doctor. This ruling is called net **neutrality**.

An ISP can't let one customer use up all of its "bandwidth" (the capacity of the Internet connection to carry **data**), and so it is allowed to put a maximum cap on the speed at which data flows to a customer. Throttling is when the ISP restricts the passage of certain types of data to ensure that their Internet service is not hogged by one kind of user, such as people streaming TV shows in the evening.

Instead of downloading the entire file for playback, audio and video is sent as a constant stream to your device. The signal is buffered, which means a few seconds or minutes of content are stored in advance before play begins. If the stream slows or stops, the buffer ensures the song or video continues uninterrupted while the connection is restored.

INTERNET ACRONYMS

Mbps (megabits per second): the speed of an Internet connection

URL (Uniform Resource Locator): a web address to you and me

IP address: a unique number given to every access point to the Internet

DNS (Domain Name Servers): the computers that contain all the URLs and IPs

TCP (Transmission Control Protocol): the rules that govern how computers share data through Internet connections

HTTP (HyperText Transfer Protocol): the rules that govern what a web page looks like

WPA (WiFi Protected Access): the preferred security system used by WiFi connections, superseding the older WEP (Wired Equivalent Privacy) system

DUMB PIPES VS SMART PIPES

The first plans for the Internet were to use what have become known as "dumb pipes." The idea is that Internet connections act like water pipes—data flows through them according to their capacity, rather than the type of data. It is now possible to have networks made of "smart pipes" which prioritize data. A smart pipe is useful for managing Internet traffic but it also makes it possible to create faster private networks within the Internet for paying customers to use.

IS ALL DATA EQUAL?

The United States recently passed laws which allowed the creation of private networks within the Internet. They would make game and video streaming services work better but rival services would be blocked. Is this a good development? Is the Internet meant to work this way?

ATTENTION ECONOMY

The impact of computing and telecommunications has been so rapid that it's hard to comprehend its effects as they occur. A simple way of understanding the big picture is as an "attention economy." We pay for services with our attention, and online services sell our attention to advertisers. Anything that gets our attention is worth something to someone. Let's give that idea some attention.

MESSAGING PARADOX

Sending and receiving messages has never been easier. First there was email, then SMS, and now there are any number of messaging apps that connect us with friends, relatives, school, and work. However, early on in the communications revolution, the messaging paradox became apparent. This says: it is so easy to send messages that a person receives them faster than they can read them. Therefore most communications are ignored. Messaging is so efficient that important information doesn't get through. Eh?

GAMES AND GOSSIP

The Internet and the World Wide Web that followed were built to make it easier to share information—and they were very successful. After about 25 years of the Web being widely available, it's now clear what kind of information we share. We like to talk about ourselves, gossip about other people, and play games with each other. Technology may be changing but how we interact with each other hasn't really altered for thousands of years.

The reason why unwanted messages are called spam is a bit of a mystery. The best suggestion is that the term comes from a Monty Python sketch (1980s computer geeks liked this kind of comedy). The sketch involves a café menu which features nothing but a canned meat called spam. The diners' conversation is regularly interrupted by several Vikings at the next table singing, "Spam, spam, spam, spam!" Unwanted email drowns out conversations in the same way.

INFLUENCERS

Humans devote a lot of attention to gossiping, or spreading news about other people. A celebrity is someone everyone knows, even though we've never actually met them. The reason why we like celebrities is because we can gossip about them, even with complete strangers. Social media has a new kind of celebrity called an "influencer," who gets our attention by sharing details about their lives. They get paid to tell us about their stuff.

WHO'S WHO?

TROLLS

A troll is a Norse monster that spends most of its time disguised as a rock. At night it emerges to spread fear and alarm, steal children, and eat all the food (and sometimes the children). The term "troll" is more often applied nowadays to anonymous voices on the Internet who like to grab people's attention by being rude and picking arguments. It is very hard to ignore either kind of troll.

WHAT'S WHAT?

FOMO

The attention economy relies on another human characteristic called FOMO, which means "fear of missing out." This fear compels people to check for new updates on the news, social media, or messaging. Some people like being left alone, but others feel they need to be involved with whatever is going on. There is always something happening on social media, so you never need to feel left out. But do you have time to view it all?

The light from the **LED** screens of phones, tablets, and computer displays contains a lot of blue light that helps the screens look bright and sharp. Our brains may mistake artificial blue light for daylight. To feel properly sleepy, we need darkness, and giving frequent attention to bright screens could be making us lose valuable sleep. That's important because getting a good night's sleep is very strongly linked with good mental and physical health.

SOCIAL MEDIA BUBBLE

Our online social groups are made up of people we like and agree with—just like in the real world. Your social media services show you things they know you already like and filter out stuff that your past clicks have revealed you don't like. As a result, social media creates a bubble, or "echo chamber" where your ideas are not challenged and you become disconnected from many of the people around you.

SCREEN ADDICTION

One of the innovations of social media is the "like" button. That is a valuable piece of information for the attention economy. Every like we get makes us happy. So we look at our device again, perhaps like and share a few things, and check if our posts have received any more likes. It can become second nature: we do it without realizing and it means we give less attention to the people around us.

Most devices offer the option to turn off services at a certain point in the day, blocking messages and notifications. Some devices will also alter the color of their screens to match the time, becoming less bright and blue in the evenings. It is generally a good idea to put a screen away around an hour before you intend to go to sleep. Read a book instead (like this one).

WHAT'S WHAT?

EFFICIENCY MODEL

The attention economy has driven the growth of the Web for the last decade, but the system is beginning to fail. We can only look at one (or two) screens at once and we ignore a lot of what we see. The smart thinking is that the online economy will opt for efficiency, which means we will soon start paying for online services in the same way we subscribe to TV channels. How much would you pay for social media?

ATTENTION CITIZENS!

The Chinese government uses a Social Credit System to encourage good citizenship. Paying bills on time and disposing of trash in the proper way earns people social credits, which are visible on social media and posted in public view in some villages. Being in debt or in trouble with the police sees your credits reduced. People with low social credit scores are barred from certain jobs and cannot access services such as flights or high-speed rail.

TIME OR MONEY?

Which system do you prefer, a free supply of internet services where if you view enough ads and behave well you get to access exclusive deals, or an Internet service where you pay for what you use?

PEER-TO-PEER

The Internet was set up to share data such as software and databases between computers. Today, the range of data has diversified from emoji messages to live video feeds. However, the setup is still the same as 50 years ago, and some people aren't happy with the amount of control other people have over how they share data online. What if everyone online were peers, or equals, and sharing was P2P or peer-to-peer, with no one in control?

CLIENT COMPUTER

The traditional model of the Internet is for devices, like your phone or laptop, to be a "client computer." Clients connect to a central server, which acts as a gateway to other clients on the network. The servers are owned by ISPs and they have control of what gets to your computer or not. In a P2P network, every device has the same level of access. There is no server with greater control over what data goes where.

NAPSTER

In 1999, P2P technology was used to allow Web-connected clients to behave as if they were on a P2P network and share files without the ISP having control. The first P2P file-sharer was Napster, which handled music files. You searched for a favorite song, and the Napster application connected you to a computer that had it, and you copied the file—for free! The recording industry was not happy and Napster was shut down.

The original vision of the World Wide Web was for every connected device to be both a client and server. Tim Berners-Lee imagined that every user of the Web would contribute content to the web of knowledge. This turned out to be only partially true. Although there is incredible scope to put self-created content on the Web, most of us consume what the Web has to offer, in terms of its video content, news feeds, and gaming services.

The next innovation was a sharing system called BitTorrent. Instead of sharing a file between two computers, hundreds of computers shared small chunks of files with hundreds of others. Computers with only a partial copy of the file were able to share that with peers that held other parts. With dozens of peers working together, BitTorrent makes it possible for an entire HD movie to be downloaded in a few minutes. The movie industry was not happy.

WHAT'S WHAT?

JAILBREAKING

Phones and gaming consoles are programmed so only software purchased through the manufacturer will work on them. Hackers use a "jailbreak" tool to free the device from the restrictions by altering fundamental bits of software. Hackers jailbreak gaming consoles so they can play "homebrew," or games they've developed themselves.

STREAMING KILLS PIRACY

Ten years ago, more than half of Internet traffic was from P2P file sharing. Sharing pirated music, movies, and software was losing their creators a lot of money. Today the figure for P2P file sharing is more like 3 percent. So what happened? Most file sharers were happy to pay to listen and watch, but they couldn't do so online. Streaming services like Spotify and Netflix have made entertainment available and so reduced the demand for pirated content.

IS PIRATING EVER RIGHT?

BitTorrent did not create sharing of music, games, and movies, but it did make it faster and more efficient. If you were never going to buy a product anyway, would using a free pirate copy be wrong?

IDENTITY CRIME

Literature is full of stories where characters take on someone else's identity. Some are hilarious, while others are tense and terrifying. But no one could actually steal your identity, could they? In real life, taking on someone's identity would be tricky, but in the online space it's easy for a criminal to pretend to be you. Online you are just as responsible for your actions as you are in the real world, so how is your identity protected?

WHAT IS YOUR IDENTITY?

You don't add up to much really. Just your name, birthplace, birthday, and address. To prove who you are, you will need a bill with your address or passport or other photo ID. Then to access your stuff you need passwords, an email address, or phone number. That's about it really!

BIOMETRICS

A human can match you to your photo in a fraction of a second. "Biometrics" are the measurements of your face or other body parts so a computer can do that same job. After about the age of 12, the relationship between certain body features becomes fixed, such as the shapes and relative positions of the eyes, nose, and mouth, so even as you age, your biometrics stay the same.

KNOW YOUR BIOMETRICS

Here are some examples of how your biometrics can be used for security.

Fingerprint (and palm print): Used to unlock phones

Facial recognition: Used in passports and to unlock phones

Iris (and retina) pattern recognition: Limited use as can be spoofed with HD image

DNA: A unique identifier at any age, although DNA scanners are far too slow for everyday ID checks

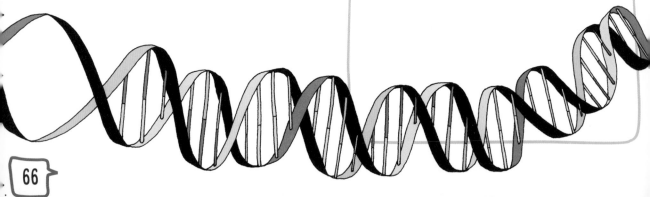

Voice activation is likely to become the dominant way we control our devices and search the Web over the next few years. We already use it to operate smart speakers and other Web-enabled assistants. If the device can understand what you are saying, it can also identify your voice. Will we be at risk of voice theft in the future?

WHAT'S WHAT?

SYNTHETIC IDENTITY

A new development in identity crime is for criminals to create a completely false identity out of scraps of information from real people. The credit agencies which record everyone's financial details have no record of this fake person, so they just create a new one so banks can lend to them. When the fraud is revealed it can cause problems for innocent people who have names and addresses similar to the fake identity.

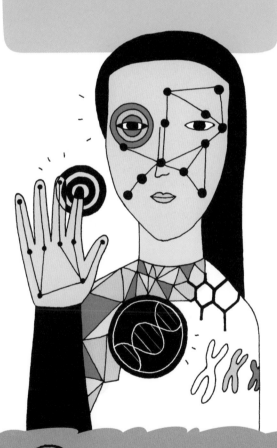

PROTECT YOUR IDENTITY

Here are a few ways you can protect your information further:
Shred documents with financial or personal information.
Wipe old phones and computers before selling them or throwing them away.
Ensure websites are secured with a https prefix to the address.
Don't publish identifying personal details on public social media.

SAFE SOLUTION?

Would having a single biometric ID system for everything make personal identities safer? In one way it would ensure we use unique features to prove our identity. But if this system were hacked, how would you prove you were you?

FAKE NEWS

In recent years we have become increasingly aware that not everything we see or read in the news is always true. It may be a mistake or a hoax or an attempt at a joke, or it might be a deliberate attempt to mislead. Does it matter which? By now we are so confused we do not know what is true and what is fake news.

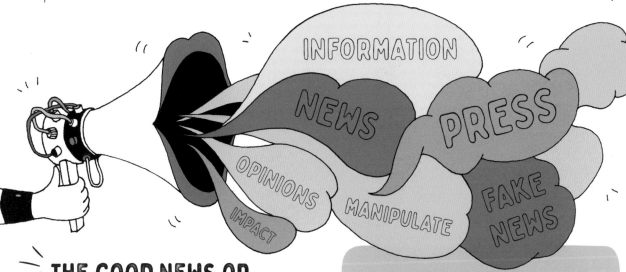

THE GOOD NEWS OR THE BAD NEWS?

People get news from newspapers, websites, or television stations that reflect their own view of the world. They avoid news outlets that contradict the way they understand things to be. They believe rival news sources at best have incorrect views, and at worst are deliberately skewing facts. Competition for readers and viewers is fierce, so news providers must appeal to a target audience and tell them news in a way they want to hear it. But is any of it really the news?

A large number of people find out about world events from friends sharing news on social media. Social media sites help out by suggesting stories that are similar to the ones people have already seen. This creates an echo chamber, where the social group repeats news and views, which may be very different to the stories being shared among other circles of friends online.

FAKE NEWS SITES

Why would anyone make a website that looked like a news provider? Many of these sites are satirical, using comedy to poke fun at real events. However, some sites deliberately make up false stories to influence people's thinking. In the 2016 US presidential election, fake stories about Donald Trump and his opponent, Hillary Clinton, were more widely read than real ones. Strangely, as a result, the real news media then started to report about all the fake news!

Fooling a few people with fake news might seem harmless but its real purpose is to sow doubt and confusion in an attempt to destabilize a society. Once a society becomes used to some news items being faked, it becomes easier for governments to deny real events. Instead these can be explained as just more fake news. This form of complex planned deception is sometimes described by the Russian word *maskirovka*, meaning "masked."

WHAT'S WHAT?

DEEPFAKE VIDEO

Can you believe your eyes? It has been possible to doctor photos for many decades but video has always been a true record of an event. However "deepfake" techniques are making it possible to merge a person's face onto someone else's body in a video using an artificial intelligence system.

ARE WE TOO INFLUENCED BY JOURNALISTS?

A lot of broadcast and online news is based around journalists discussing an event, setting out what they think happened, why it happened, and what might happen next. Do these opinions help us understand the news or is something else going on?

CYBERWAR

Victory in war requires a decisive weapon or strategy of some kind. In ancient days, military leaders would target a castle or other stronghold and destroy food supplies. In more recent years, the focus shifted to bridges, factories, and supply routes. Today, war has entered the cybersphere. Whichever side wins online will win on the battlefield as well. Hacking skills might just save a country from defeat.

Military computer networks are more secure than websites and public-facing computers, so hacking attacks should have little impact on them. However, the civilian infrastructure, such as the electricity grid, traffic management, and financial system, are also targets in cyberwarfare. Turning off the power and money supply and simply cutting a territory's connection to the Internet would cause chaos and confusion that an enemy could capitalize on.

CYBER ATTACKS

The Internet itself was born out of a military project to develop a communications network that would work even when its cables and routers became damaged. Now, enemy cybersoldiers use hacking techniques to bring the network down from the inside. They no longer need to target hardware, like cables. They release viruses and worms which block the communication systems, making it harder for a military command to get information, process data, and send out orders. This is just as effective as cutting a wire.

FANCY BEAR

Fancy Bear is a group of hackers working for the GRU, the Russian military intelligence service. They have been shown to be involved in several cyberattacks on governments and international organizations, including meddling in the US, French, and German elections and trying to stop drug-cheat Russian athletes from being banned from the Olympics.

EMP WEAPONS

An EMP (electromagnetic pulse) weapon releases a powerful burst of radiation which overloads all the low-voltage electronics in the area, rendering them useless. A nuclear explosion releases an EMP (and causes a lot more damage!). One strategy would be to explode a nuke high in the air to knock out the electronics below while minimizing other damage. "E-bombs," or non-nuclear EMP weapons, can produce a targetable beam to knock out military installations.

The design of a rival military's E-bombs would be a valuable piece of intelligence. Cyberwarfare meets spying when it comes to stealing military secrets. Although they do not admit it, China appears to be adept at this. Most of their fast jet fighters appear to be close copies of US and Russian models.

MEDDLING

Cyberwarfare need not be deadly. In fact, some would argue that the world powers are in a near-constant cyberbattle even during peacetime. The visible front of this secret conflict is the use of techniques such as fake news to destabilize the social cohesion of a rival country. For example, social media can be used to stir up division in one country and to promote a good image of another, or to influence how an electorate views a particular politician.

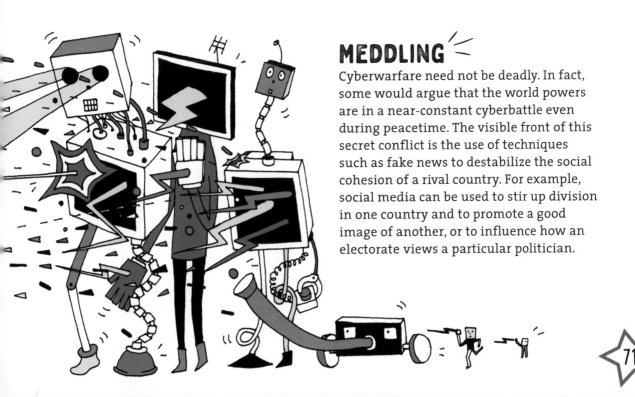

STUXNET

In 2010, a computer worm called Stuxnet was discovered when it infected the networks at Iran's nuclear facilities. Stuxnet supposedly infected 200,000 devices and took control of sensitive machines so that they destroyed themselves. No one has claimed responsibility for the Stuxnet attack. Some countries have been suspected, including Israel and the United States, who doubted Iran's intentions for deveolping nuclear fuel. But we cannot say for sure.

Stuxnet was so successful because it made use of not one but four serious flaws that made systems vulnerable to hacking. All were so-called "zero-day flaws," problems that the engineers, manufacturers and owners of the software or hardware do not know exist and therefore have done nothing to remove them. Cyberweapons like Stuxnet rely on zero-day flaws as a way through cyberdefences, but once used, the flaws are revealed and the weapon becomes useless.

ESTONIA ATTACKED

One of the first well-publicized cyberattacks occurred in Estonia in April 2007. Russian hackers caused denial of services attacks that knocked out government ministries, broadcasters, and banks. For two days, the country was thrown into chaos, with airports and train stations closed, ATMs out of action, and fluctuating power supplies. News and political websites were defaced with anti-Estonian slogans and pictures. Estonia and her allies believed an attack of such sophistication must have had official military control.

TITAN RAIN

The largest cyberattack ever recorded is codenamed Titan Rain. It has seen US government institutions and high-tech defense companies that work for them attacked multiple times for more than 15 years. You will probably not have heard of this cyberwarfare campaign because it is meant to be unseen, using quiet espionage to steal secrets from the US military and NASA. It is assumed that the Titan Rain attacks are coming from China but there is no direct evidence.

WANNACRY

In 2017, a ransomware attack called WannaCry caused mayhem across the world. The worm had its worst effects in organizations that used a large number of computers that were not updated regularly. Victims included the UK's National Health Service, Renault factories in France, and Russia's Ministry of Internal Affairs. Thousands of computers became locked unless a ransom was paid. The worm was traced to North Korea and might have been an attempt to raise money or simply cause disruption.

WHAT'S WHAT?

GREAT FIREWALL OF CHINA

China has complete control over what data gets into the Internet serving the Chinese mainland. This is achieved using a system nicknamed "the Great Firewall of China." The Chinese government uses the Great Firewall to prevent cyberattacks but also to censor Web content from outside China, blocking anything that makes China's rulers look bad.

The best defense against cyberattacks is to switch off connections from outside the country. In most places, such an act would render services useless, but the Russian Internet, Runet, is designed to keep working when cut off from the rest of the world.

SHOULD HACKING BE A WAR CRIME?

There are various international treaties and agreements about what is allowed in war and what weapons and tactics are not. For example, it is a war crime to use chemical weapons or to destroy cultural artefacts on purpose. Should anything to do with cyberwarfare be prohibited by the laws of war?

CRYPTOCURRENCIES

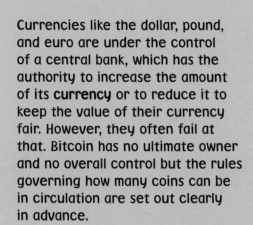

Hacking is all about working out new ways to do something, or how to use old technology in a new way. As we've seen, that goes beyond computing into many areas of life. One of the biggest triumphs is hacking money itself. The result is bitcoin, a form of money that has no one in charge and that is always traded in public in a completely fair way, although no one knows who owns any of it.

Currencies like the dollar, pound, and euro are under the control of a central bank, which has the authority to increase the amount of its **currency** or to reduce it to keep the value of their currency fair. However, they often fail at that. Bitcoin has no ultimate owner and no overall control but the rules governing how many coins can be in circulation are set out clearly in advance.

CRYPTOCURRENCY

Bitcoin is the leading example of a cryptocurrency. Based on its name, you might assume a cryptocurrency is one set up to be used in secret by people wanting to avoid detection. Bitcoin does allow for this, but a cryptocurrency really gets its name from the strong forms of cryptography used to secure the release of new coins, verify transactions, and maintain an absolutely true record so that everyone can trust the process.

MINING FOR BITCOIN

For Bitcoins to exist, they have to be 'mined' by using a computer to solve a tricky cryptological puzzle. The process is one of trial and error, so the speed that the miner earns bitcoins depends on how many processors they devote to the task. As the number of miners increases, the puzzles become harder so that bitcoins are released at a regular rate. Today, bitcoin miners have to use supercomputers and must make 200 million billion attempts to solve each puzzle.

The mining system ensures that bitcoin has value by creating scarcity. As the number of bitcoins increases, the rate at which miners get paid goes down. When there are 210 million bitcoins, which will happen around 2140, miners will get nothing in return for solving puzzles. Bitcoin will eventually run out, and that makes it different from every other currency. Some argue that it disqualifies it from really being a currency. Instead it is a commodity like gold or precious jewels.

WHO'S WHO?

SATOSHI NAKAMOTO

Bitcoin was created by the computer scientist Satoshi Nakamoto, who released the software needed for it to work on January 3rd 2009. Nakamoto made the first bitcoin transaction on January 12th. No one knows who the mastermind might be.

BLOCKCHAIN

Every transaction made with bitcoin is recorded in a public record called the "blockchain." This isn't held on a single central server but distributed over a peer-to-peer network of bitcoin miners. Every ten minutes or so, the processing work done by the miners creates a new block which records all the transactions that happened in those ten minutes. That encrypted block is shared on the network, so the entire world knows when each bitcoin was traded.

BITCOIN BUBBLE?

Bitcoin's success is an example of a speculative bubble. **Speculators** buy bitcoin not to use it but because they believe that its value will increase. If there is demand from other people to buy bitcoin, then the price will certainly go up. But what happens if the only people who want bitcoin are speculators? Eventually the demand will fall away. It might turn out that bitcoins are not really worth anything at all.

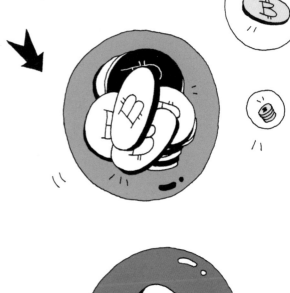

The first person to buy something with bitcoins spent 10,000 on two takeout pizzas in 2010. In 2011, one bitcoin was worth around $0.30. By 2017, the value had gone up to $19,666! While bitcoins can be used to buy normal things, people usually purchase them as an investment, selling them when their value is high. Owners access their bitcoins using a private number key. If that key is lost, the bitcoins are also lost—forever. Around 20 percent of all bitcoins have been lost so far.

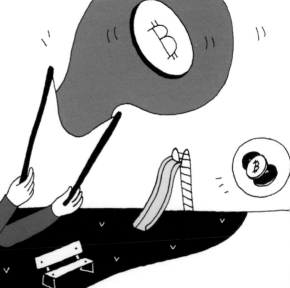

In spite of the worries about a bitcoin bubble, it seems that there is demand to use bitcoin as a currency. However, that demand is not entirely good news. It is estimated that nearly half of all bitcoin transactions are being used to buy something illegal. The anonymous nature of the blockchain also makes it easier to launder money, where the proceeds from crime are passed through a fake company so they appear as profits from a business.

WHAT'S WHAT?

SMART CONTRACT

Blockchain technology could be used in other areas, such as signing, enforcing and settling contracts. In a "smart contract," Person 1 agrees to pay Person 2 for a service. Person 1 deposits the fee as bitcoin into the blockchain. When Person 2 completes the service, the fee goes to them. If they fail to complete the service, the fee goes back to person 1. The blockchain simply replaces the lawyers and accountants who would normally handle such contracts—and does it for free!

? IS BITCOIN BETTER?

Imagine if bitcoin replaced the current currency completely. Would it be better? Think about how it might be fairer, clearer, or more efficient than an old currency—or how it might end up being worse.

THE DARK WEB

What does a name like "dark web" mean to you? Does it sound intriguing or frightening? The dark web is the section of the Internet that's hidden from public view. To get in, a user needs special software and knowledge. Once inside they are anonymous and their activity is harder to trace. The dark web sounds like a perfect set up for a hacker but it is also where you find serious criminals.

DEEP WEB

The dark web is just a small part of the "deep web"—that is everything that's contained on Web-enabled servers but isn't indexed by search engines. As a result, Google, Bing, and the others don't know it's there, and you can't access it without the exact link. The deep web is composed mostly of innocuous private content, such as webmail messages and online financial services, plus content that is behind a "paywall," meaning you have to pay to access it.

No own knows for sure, but it is estimated that the deep web makes up more than 99 percent of the total web. The tiny part that we can see is called the "surface web." Even that contains 4.5 billion recorded websites but the deep web is thought to contain up to 600 times as much information.

DARKNETS

Remember the dark web is the part that is deliberately hidden from us. This includes things like peer-to-peer networks distributing files and maintaining the bitcoin blockchain. However, within that there are also "darknets," which are private regions of a network, deliberately walled off from the rest of the Web. The darknets are the main focus of attention when it comes to the dark web. Why do the users want to stay hidden? Surely it can't all be completely harmless?

TOR

The name of the most famous darknet—Tor —comes from "the onion router" because every connection to and from the network is bounced around at random among a mind-boggling array of nodes (like the many layers of an onion). Tor was originally developed by the US military in the 1990s as a means of communicating in perfect secrecy. While using a Tor browser is legal, more than half of the activity on the Tor network is illegal.

DREAD PIRATE ROBERTS

In 2011, every conceivable illegal service was for sale on Silk Road—a dark web market. A huge effort was made to capture its founder, known as Dread Pirate Roberts. This name comes from the 1980s movie *The Princess Bride*, referring to the most feared criminal in the world. In 2013, American Ross Ulbricht was exposed as Dread Pirate Roberts and sentenced to life in prison.

Tor is not completely foolproof. Plug-ins can reveal the true IP of a device. Also, while connections are encrypted inside Tor, they must leave the system to connect to a surface web service, like a search engine. The connection becomes public as it leaves Tor. Whoever owns the exit node (the device connecting the Tor web to the surface web) could monitor your activity.

ARE DARKNETS ALWAYS BAD?

Should darknet software like Tor be banned? If so how would you go about doing so? Would it be a criminal offense to own software or to use it? Could darknet software ever be used for good, perhaps by persecuted people?

THE INTERNET OF THINGS

The early Internet was an "internetwork" that transferred data between computers. Then came the Web—the Internet was all about connecting people, exchanging news, views, and cat videos. So where next? In 2003, 99 percent of connections to the Internet were made by a person. Today people make less than half of connections—the rest are made autonomously by devices. In the 2020s, machines will outnumber us by six to one. Welcome to the Internet of Things.

EMBEDDED TECHNOLOGY

Where once a computer was a beige box connected to a keyboard and monitor, they are now embedded in all kinds of places around the home, in the built environment, and throughout the natural world. They are controllers, recorders, and sensors that send and receive signals to and from the Internet. One day, the machines that surround us will be able to use that data to perform tasks independently.

HOME TECHNOLOGY

Technology has begun to impact our home life as we connect our homes to the Internet. It is now possible to remote control home settings while we are out, to adjust the heating, cook food, or even answer the door. When are home, some houses know where everyone is, adjusting the lighting, heating, and sounds in each room according to our personal settings.

An Internet-linked device might soon be able to perform automated tasks on our behalf. For example, a smart fridge could record what food it contains and learn how quickly different items are used. It could then place regular orders automatically so you never run out. The fridge could shop for a menu of meals that you've selected and access your diary to buy extra for days when more people are home.

WHAT'S WHAT?

WEB OF THINGS

Much of the Internet of Things involves meaningless streams of data that we do not understand or don't really want to. Like the early days of the Internet, it is all about data moving around. However, we will want to interact with some "things"—a car, house, or our robot pet, for example—and we will do that using the same technology that allows us to interact with each other over the Web.

In the house of the future, the smart toilet will bristle with sensors that analyze the chemicals you leave behind. This data could be sent to a health tracker app to create a fitness plan and to the fridge to buy foods to suit your metabolism. The toilet's records could be shared with your doctor along with other health data to offer early warnings of disease. If it really needed to, an Internet toilet could call you an ambulance!

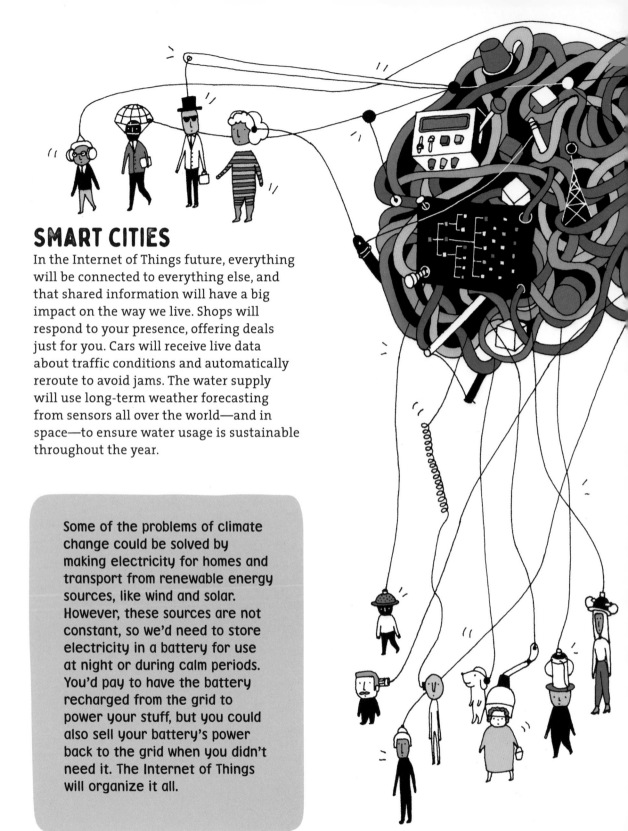

SMART CITIES

In the Internet of Things future, everything will be connected to everything else, and that shared information will have a big impact on the way we live. Shops will respond to your presence, offering deals just for you. Cars will receive live data about traffic conditions and automatically reroute to avoid jams. The water supply will use long-term weather forecasting from sensors all over the world—and in space—to ensure water usage is sustainable throughout the year.

Some of the problems of climate change could be solved by making electricity for homes and transport from renewable energy sources, like wind and solar. However, these sources are not constant, so we'd need to store electricity in a battery for use at night or during calm periods. You'd pay to have the battery recharged from the grid to power your stuff, but you could also sell your battery's power back to the grid when you didn't need it. The Internet of Things will organize it all.

WHAT'S WHAT?

BIG DATA

"Big data" is the idea that the more information we have about something the better we understand it. Narrow AIs search for patterns in data that are beyond human abilities, which allow AIs to manage complex systems. The Internet of Things will bring all those complex systems together to make a system of systems. It is suggested that human intelligence grows out of big data in the brain. Perhaps the Internet of Things will develop a strong AI from handling big data.

ARTIFICIAL INTELLIGENCE

A lot of the projected benefits of the Internet of Things relies on artificial intelligence (AI). There are two ways of looking at AI. Narrow AI learns how to do one thing really well, often better than a human can, but can't learn to do something outside of its programming. Strong AI, by contrast, knows what it doesn't know and figures out what it needs to learn to achieve a goal. In this way, strong AI (which only exists in science fiction) is like a human's EI (evolved intelligence).

Are you concerned about AI? Will super-smart computers take over? Perhaps not in the way that you might see in films. Instead of an army of robots ruling Earth, AI might take over because no human understands what it does. We could turn it off but then nothing would work.

DO YOU WANT TO LIVE ON AUTOPILOT?

The Internet of Things could think for you and run a lot of your day-to-day life on automatic. Would you like not having to organize so much, or would you feel the technology restricted the way you lived?

COMPUTING THE FUTURE

Computing has a problem. Throughout its history, the speed and power of computers has only ever increased. Fast processors once only found in cutting-edge facilities are now in all our devices. Today, a pocket-sized device can connect us with anyone anywhere on the planet—and even in orbit! However, our desire for more and more processing power cannot be met forever. We will have to find a new way of computing.

MOORE'S LAW

In 1965, Gordon Moore, the head of the Intel microchip company, predicted that the number of components on a microchip, and so the amount of data a computer could process, would double every 18 months. So far Moore's Law has proved broadly correct. If there were no limits, by the 2050s a computer chip would have the processing power of every human brain on Earth working together. As it stands, Moore's law is expected to be broken by 2025.

As you might expect, hackers try to make computers run faster than their original design allows. This approach is called "overclocking," and hackers do it to make cheap hardware work as well as an expensive computer or to make games and other graphical content work better. There is a downside, however. Overclocked microchips use a lot of electricity and get very hot unless extra cooling is added, so their lifespan is generally short.

QUANTUM COMPUTING

A silicon transistor holds information by being switched on (1) or off (0). Quantum computing would do away with silicon and record information using the quantum properties of an atom or molecule—their spin direction, magnetism, and electrical charge. A particle's quantum properties are hard to pin down and so are best understood in terms of chance. For example, the chance that the spin direction is "up" might be 0.7 and so "down" would be 0.3. The on–off switch on a silicon chip can only hold one piece or "bit" of information, a 1 or 0. A quantum bit, or "qubit," holds two pieces of information (0.7 and 0.3) at the same time. A 32-bit computer handles 32 bits of information at a time, but a 32-qubit computer holds 4,294,967,296 bits at a time. You can see how quantum computing might make very powerful processors in the future.

True quantum computing has not yet been achieved. Research projects must shield quantum devices from heat, light, radiation, and magnetism and keep them in a vacuum at -459°F (colder than space). If it can be made to work, a quantum computer wouldn't necessarily work faster than today's supercomputers, but it could handle so much information at once, it should be able to solve problems that would take a normal computer millions of years to process.

WHAT'S WHAT?

TRANSISTOR

A microchip has millions of tiny silicon switches called transistors which work as switches by creating a tiny barrier to an electric current. Moore's Law has proved true because computer scientists have reduced that gap from 10 millionths of a meter in the 1970s to 5 nanometers today. Any smaller than that and electricity will start leaking across the gap.

UNLIMITED COMPUTING?

What would you do if there was no limit to computing power? You could create an entirely virtual world in which to have adventures. Back in the real world Big Data and AI keeps your body properly fed, clean, and healthy. Does that sound fun?

GENE HACKING

Hacking began with model railways and produced the biggest computer and software companies in the world. Hackers have impacted many fields from journalism to art, and even the way money works. However, the most significant hacks in the future might be made to our own bodies. The technology exists to hack DNA to fix a problem or give your body a new ability—and change the genes that generations to come will inherit. But should we hack genes? Is it right?

CLONING

Cloning is a generic hack where a baby animal is created which is identical to its single parent. The most famous clone is Dolly the Sheep who was born in 1996. Cloning humans is illegal—and may not even be possible—not least because most cloning attempts end in severe developmental problems. Dolly was the only survivor of 277 attempts to produce a clone.

CRISPR

The main gene-hacking technique is called CRISPR Cas9. It uses a defense system used by bacteria to cut up virus DNA. The CRISPR system has been hacked so it can be reprogrammed to cut any DNA, including human DNA, at a very precise place. A new bit of DNA can be added to reconnect the severed ends, adding in new genetic information and thus hacking the gene so it works in a different way.

CRISPR is used to create synthetic organisms by editing the genomes (the full set of genes) of simple organisms like bacteria or yeast. Synthetic organisms are engineered to do a specific experimental task. A synthetic bacteria could be a toxin sensor that glows when it finds poison in water. A synthetic algae could make gasoline from sunlight instead of sugar.

It is possible to buy CRISPR kits through the mail. Biohackers have tried to use them to change their own bodies, injecting themselves with genes that change skin color, give defenses against diseases, or make muscles grow. While CRISPR works on single-celled creatures like bacteria, it is unlikely to have much effect on a human body, which has 30 trillion cells. It is illegal to use CRISPR on sperm or egg cells because that would lead to hacked genes creating a genetically modified baby.

WHAT'S WHAT?

A GENE

A gene is a piece of DNA (deoxyribonucleic acid), a long chemical carrying the genetic code needed to build a body. A single gene carries the code to make one protein that makes up DNA. A gene is also a characteristic that can be inherited, such as hair and skin color. Genetics is the study of how the first idea of a gene relates to the second.

STEM CELL THERAPY

Every cell in the body is specialized—we have blood cells, bone cells, and muscle cells, for example. They all develop from a powerful starter cell, the stem cell, but once specialized, the cell cannot change to another form. Doctors have figured out how to hack certain body cells to turn them back into these stem cells. Stem cells could then be used to grow new organs, heal nerves, and fix other injuries that are currently incurable.

SHOULD LIFE BE EDITED?

Would you want to edit your own genes? What kinds of features would you fix? Should there be any limits on what genes can and cannot be altered? Genes are inherited, so any changes you make could be passed to your children.

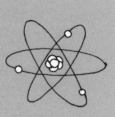

PROS AND CONS

So now that we've taken a tour of the world of computer technology and hacking, are you excited by the future promised by big data, quantum computing, and AI? Do you want to know more about cryptocurrencies, blockchains, and the Internet of Things? Or are you terrified of the risk of hacking attacks and confused by fake news? There is a lot to take in and weigh up. It might help to think about the different ways we can understand morality and ethics, the systems that we use to divide good from bad.

CONSEQUENCES

One school of ethics can be summed up by the phrase, "All's well that ends well." The focus of this way of understanding good and bad is the consequence of someone's actions. Imagine two twins driving recklessly. One crashes and injures a pedestrian, while the other parks without incident. Have they both been equally wrong despite the second driver causing no harm? Did the crashing driver do more wrong than his twin?

Utilitarianism is an ethics system that treats positive and negative consequences like a sum. It says that the idea of morality is to increase the positive consequences (happiness) and minimize negative ones (pain), and so every deed should be judged on its ability to do that. Taking this literally, however, we might find problems. Your happiness could be boosted a little by a gift of $10. Say the richest person in the world has $70 billion, enough to give everyone else $10. Would the pain caused by that person losing their money be outweighed by the happiness of 7 billion people getting free money?

Perhaps a better form of utilitarianism is summed up by the harm principle. Instead of having a very long list of behaviors that are agreed to be good, you can do whatever you like as long as it does not cause any harm to someone else. However, are you allowed to harm yourself? And is it ever possible to harm yourself without harming someone else at least a little?

DUTY

Being moral means doing the right thing by other people even if you suffer as a result. It is what you do that counts as good or bad, not what happens when you do it. Good behaviors come from duties, which are things that are self-evidently good, such as helping people in pain. Duties do not include things that are just nice to have, such as pleasure or wealth.

VIRTUE

This is a very old way of understanding good and bad that dates back to the days of the ancient Greeks. Behaving in a good way relies on a person having good qualities, such as generosity, kindness, and patience. Behaving badly uses bad qualities and leads to unhappiness. But virtue ethics can allow a person to link whatever makes them feel good inside as the right thing to do. Is what makes you feel good always the right thing to do?

RELATIVISM

This set of ideas tells us that good and bad changes as society changes and learns more about the world and how to control it in useful ways. Anything goes as long as it benefits society as a whole. If you can get away with a behavior without society condemning you for it, then that is a good behavior. This means that what was a crime in the past may be allowed today, and what might be normal behavior in one country is not in another.

MIND MAP

You've reached the end of the book and now know a lot about hacking, but what do you think about it? After learning about different moral codes, do you think it's right? Or is it ultimately wrong? Are some aspects good? I can't tell you the answer, because there isn't one! You have to make your own informed opinon, but now you have the tools to do just that. This mind map is a starting point to building the big picture of hacking and online technology. Every subject seems to lead to another, and every question answered ends up with more things to ask. I always think that's what makes this stuff so interesting, the way a wide array of subjects all seems to link together. Makes you think, doesn't it? So, now you have the information, what will your opinion be?

ACTIVISM

WHISTLE-BLOWING

LIFE HACK

GENE HACK

VIRUS

MALWARE

TROJAN

PHREAKING

HACKING

TELEPHONE

SMS

EMAIL

THE INTERNET

PHISHING

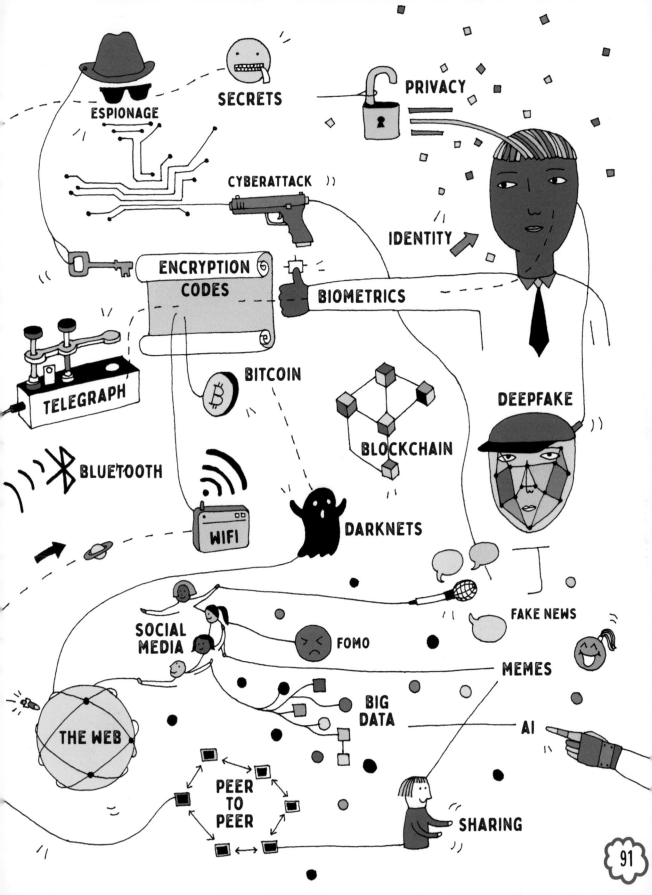

ESPIONAGE

SECRETS

PRIVACY

CYBERATTACK

IDENTITY

ENCRYPTION CODES

BIOMETRICS

DEEPFAKE

TELEGRAPH

BITCOIN

BLOCKCHAIN

BLUETOOTH

WIFI

DARKNETS

FAKE NEWS

SOCIAL MEDIA

FOMO

MEMES

AI

THE WEB

BIG DATA

PEER TO PEER

SHARING

GLOSSARY

activist a person who tries to make a change in society through their actions

algebra a system of calculation where numbers are represented by letters

algorithm a list of instructions designed to turn a starting point into an end point

anonymous to have no name or identifiable features

bit a single unit of information, normally recorded by a computer as a 1 or 0

blockchain an online record of transactions that is public and cannot be changed or doctored

browser the software application used to access and view material that is available on the World Wide Web

byte a unit of memory, made up of eight bits

CCTV (closed-circuit television), a name for security cameras where an area—a shop or street, perhaps—can be viewed on screens

cloning a system that makes a genetic copy of a living thing. The clone shares the same DNA as the original but is not an exact copy.

copyright the rule that says text, pictures, or any other creative product belongs to the person who made it, and cannot be copied without their permission

currency the system of exchange used to buy and sell things

data information, often in the form of numbers, that has been recorded in relation to something specific

encryption the process of hiding the meaning of information using codes and ciphers

ethics a set of principles that guide decision making

hardware the physical parts of a computer, including the display or screen, the keyboard, processors, memory, and power supply

infrastructure the constructions, such as roads, bridges, and tunnels, power and water supplies, and communications that allow people to move around public spaces and live normal lives

input the start point of a computer program. This could be a click of a keyboard or swipe of finger. The programming will then convert that input into an output.

intelligence in this context, referring to information collected about a rival, enemy, or competitor. The purpose of espionage, or spying, is to gather intelligence and understand what it means.

LED short for light-emitting diode, an electronic device that emits bright light when electrified. LEDs are used in flat-screen displays (and numerous other places).

life hack a technique for making a part of everyday life easier, generally using something designed for another purpose entirely

neutrality not taking sides and being balanced between one point of view and another opinion

output the end result of a computer algorithm, which could be a sound made by a speaker, or a pixel appearing on a screen

poll a survey that asks a group of people their opinion about an issue of the day, and uses the results to estimate the opinion of a much larger group, even the entire country

processor the microchip "brain" of a computer that contains the algorithms of a program and uses them to turn inputs into outputs

protocol a set of strict rules that control how computers communicate and exchange information

quantum a small packet of something. In terms of quantum physics, this relates to the way matter and energy are constructed of small packets that cannot be divided up or added to.

software the programs that control computer hardware

speculator someone who buys and sells things based on how they think their value will change in the future

surveillance a close observation of a person, recording everything they do

The Pentagon the headquarters of the US military, so named because it is located inside a giant five-sided building near Washington, D.C.

FIND OUT MORE

Now over to you. Use these resources to continue your exploration of all things hacking, coding, and computing. You can find out more in books and on websites. A computing museum will show you where all the technology came from, while games are a good place to start out as a codebreaker. Good luck!

BOOKS
There are many books written on the subject of hacking, some by hackers themselves. These ones are a good place to start.

Hacking For Dummies by Kevin Beaver; John Wiley & Sons; 2018

Ghost in the Wires: My Adventures as the World's Most Wanted Hacker by Kevin Mitnick; Little, Brown and Company; 2011

The Science of Computers
(Get Ahead in Computing) by Clive Gifford; Wayland; 2016

WEBSITES AND ONLINE ARTICLES
Where best to learn about computer hackers than on your computer?

What is Hacking?
www.bbc.co.uk/newsround/39896362

White Hat Honor Code, RØØtz
www.rØØtz.org

15 Under 15: Rising Stars in Cybersecurity
projects.csmonitor.com/hackerkids

All web addresses were correct at the time of printing. The Publishers and author cannot be held responsible for the content of the websites referred to in this book.

GAMES

You can learn more about hacking and experiment with the skills yourself with these games.

CIA code breakers
https://www.cia.gov/kids-page/games/break-the-code

Hackers, board game
https://www.thinkfun.com/products/hacker

MUSEUMS

Museums are great places to visit to discover and learn more about Hackers and computers in an interactive way.

National Cryptologic Museum, Maryland
www.cryptologicfoundation.org

Computer History Museum, California
https://www.computerhistory.org

WORKSHOPS AND HACKER EVENTS

If you've been inspired by this book to experiment with hacking then these events and workshops are for you. Just remember only white hat hacking is legal!

RØØtz Asylum; Las Vegas; Nevada; USA
www.rØØtz.org

Hak4Kids; Chicago; Illinois; USA
www.hak4kidz.com

APPS

Learn more on the go with apps which you can download to your smart phone.

The Guides, RosiMosi LLC (Android / iOS)
A curious game, full of mind-challenging puzzles which will keep you occupied for hours. Can you hack it?

A FEW FINAL QUESTIONS...

Would it be possible to hack the weather to solve climate change? We better think big, if so.

Technology is changing the way we live, but what for? Does technology help us take charge of our lives and make life better? Or are we changing the way we organize our lives to make the technology work better? The answer is not always clear. Perhaps it's a bit of both.

Does this book make you want to turn off your phone, disconnect from the web, and live off grid? How would you even go about that?

INDEX